# Praise for *Designing EduProtocols*

*Designing EduProtocols* shows teachers how thoughtful lesson design can unlock student thinking, reduce confusion, and create classrooms where learning feels purposeful, efficient, and genuinely student-centered without adding more to a teacher's already full plate.

—**Adam Moler,** social studies teacher and coauthor of *EduProtocols Field Guide: Social Studies Edition*

*Designing EduProtocols* is a refreshing, thoughtful guide that strips away clutter and overdesign, offering educators clear, practical frameworks that energize teaching, honor student learning, and make sustainable, engaging instruction feel both possible and inspiring.

—**Ariana Hernandez,** science teacher and coauthor of *EduProtocols Field Guide: Science Edition*

In *Designing EduProtocols*, Mark addresses two of the biggest challenges in education today, time and student engagement, by helping educators see their classrooms through the lens of a designer and reconnect educators to the joy of teaching.

—**Zack Kruger,** elementary principal, Lakeview Elementary, Owatonna, MN

*Designing EduProtocols* reframes teaching through the lens of intentional design, showing educators how clean, purposeful frameworks can unlock student voice, reduce burnout, and reignite the joy of learning.

—**Dominic Helmstetter,** high school teacher, Perrysburg High School

*Designing EduProtocols* empowers educators to design intentional, high-impact learning experiences using flexible, student-centered routines that work in every classroom and across all content areas, offering a practical framework that reduces preparation time, increases engagement, and supports consistent, meaningful learning for all students.

—**Christy Hewitt,** instructional coach, Florence Chapel Middle School, Spartanburg, SD

After years of modifying EduProtocols, I finally have a clear understanding of their design logic. My future adaptations will be much more strategic and purpose-driven.

—**Taryn Shears,** secondary teacher, St Patrick's College Mackay (Queensland, Australia)

In a time of teacher burnout, Mark Wallace's book *Designing EduProtocols* reignites purpose, inspires vision, and empowers educators to return to the heart of meaningful teaching that is focused on real and engaging work without all the fake frills.

—**Audra Wood,** fourth-grade teacher, Park County School District #6, Cody, WY

This book redefines instructional design by showing teachers how intentional, joyful learning experiences built with student agency at the center create balance, creativity, and lasting impact in the classroom.

—**Christina Miramontes,** middle school science teacher and coauthor of *EduProtocols Field Guide: Science Edition*

*Designing EduProtocols* prompts a critical re-evaluation of classroom design and its influence on student success. It offers a compelling argument for reconsidering traditional instructional planning methods.

—**Stephanie Dickens,** instructional coach, Rockingham County, NC

This book deepens teachers' awareness of how intentional design fuels deeper learning by stripping away distractions and over-scaffolding so students can focus on sense-making, decision-making, and expressing their own thinking, using EduProtocols as frameworks that elevate ownership and engagement.

—**Lisa Roy,** instructional coach, Chesapeake Public Schools

*Designing EduProtocols* speaks directly to the moment so many educators find themselves in right now—experienced, committed, and tired of chasing "new" strategies that don't last. Mark Wallace slows the reader down just enough to reconnect them to why they teach, how design communicates values, and what truly separates an EduProtocol from yet another activity. His journey from skeptic to designer mirrors the path of countless teachers who crave sustainability without sacrificing engagement. If you've ever felt energized by EduProtocols but unsure how to move from user to creator, this book will make you feel seen, grounded, and ready.

—**Kim Voge,** instructional leader, EduProtocols practitioner and designer

*Designing EduProtocols* respects the realities of modern classrooms while challenging educators to design smarter—not harder—through iterative, brain-compatible frameworks that increase engagement, clarity, and student ownership without adding more work.

—**Robert Mayfield,** coordinator, Language and Literacy; college instructor, San Joaquin COE; Teachers College of San Joaquin

# Designing EduProtocols

**Design Smarter. Work Less. Transform More.**

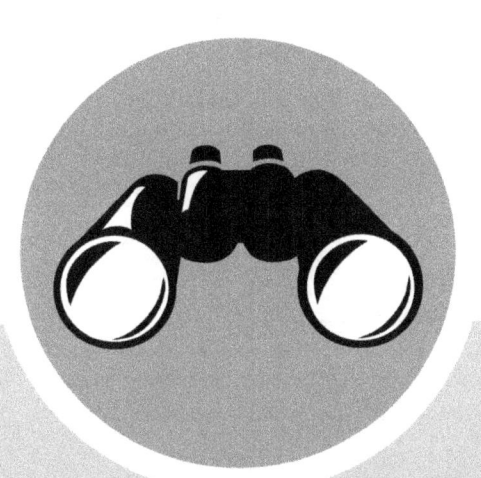

# DESIGNING
# EduProtocols®

## 8 Lesson Frames
### TO GUIDE YOUR DESIGN JOURNEY

## Mark Wallace
with Jon Corippo & Marlena Hebern

*Designing EduProtocols: 8 Lesson Frames to Guide Your Design Journey*
© 2026 Mark Wallace with Jon Corippo and Marlena Hebern

EduProtocols® is a registered trademark of Marlena Hebern and Jon Corippo.

All rights reserved. No part of this publication may be reproduced in any form or by any electronic or mechanical means, including information storage and retrieval systems, without permission in writing by the publisher, except by a reviewer who may quote brief passages in a review. For information regarding permission, contact the publisher at books@daveburgessconsulting.com.

> This book is available at special discounts when purchased in quantity for educational purposes or for use as premiums, promotions, or fundraisers. For inquiries and details, contact the publisher at books@daveburgessconsulting.com.

Published by Dave Burgess Consulting, Inc.
Vancouver, WA
DaveBurgessConsulting.com

Library of Congress Control Number: 2026933551
Paperback ISBN: 978-1-968898-15-1
Ebook ISBN: 978-1-968898-16-8

Cover and interior design by Liz Schreiter
Edited and produced by Reading List Editorial
ReadingListEditorial.com

*For Deb.*

*Innovative teaching partner of twenty-five years and a big sister along the way.*

# Contents

| | |
|---|---|
| 1 | **Section 1: The Journey** |
| 2 | Chapter 1: How I Got Here: My EP Design Story |
| 8 | Chapter 2: The Deeper Messaging Behind Design |
| 15 | Chapter 3: Design Basics from a Layman Designer |
| 22 | Chapter 4: What Makes an EduProtocol an EduProtocol? |
| 33 | Chapter 5: The Process of EduProtocol Design |
| | |
| 42 | **Section 2: 8 New EduProtocols and Their Iterative Origin Stories** |
| 43 | Chapter 6: Capitalization pARTS EduProtocol |
| 50 | Chapter 7: StoryScan EduProtocol |
| 58 | Chapter 8: Echo Chamber EduProtocol |
| 66 | Chapter 9: ReRoute EduProtocol |
| 78 | Chapter 10: Word Hunters EduProtocol |
| 87 | Chapter 11: Wordplay Factory EduProtocol |
| 95 | Chapter 12: BioBytes EduProtocol |
| 102 | Chapter 13: FlipSwitch EduProtocol |
| | |
| 111 | **Section 3: Designing Your Own EduProtocols** |
| 112 | Chapter 14: Designing Your Own EduProtocols |
| 118 | Chapter 15: Join the Movement: Become the Designer You Already Are |
| | |
| 122 | Acknowledgments |
| 125 | About Mark Wallace |
| 126 | More from Dave Burgess Consulting, Inc. |

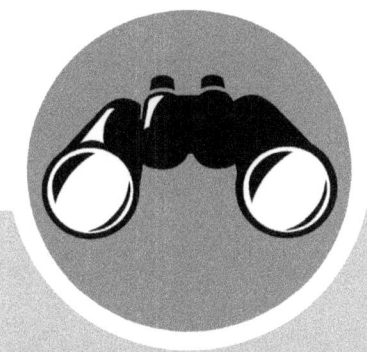

# SECTION 1
## The Journey

# Chapter 1
## How I Got Here: My EP Design Story

**I was leaving school earlier, I was feeling more energized, and my students were more engaged than ever.** This wasn't the result of a new curriculum, expensive technology, or district initiative. It began when I finally stopped ignoring my colleague Matt's enthusiasm about something he called EduProtocols.

But to understand how I got here, I need to take you back eighteen years.

## The Rise of Complexity

For the first ten years of my career, I was either single or newly married, and I had gotten away with working weekends, early mornings, and evenings. Taking my work home was assumed. If you had asked any teaching colleague how they were doing during those years, they would likely have responded with the same answer: "Busy." Finding energizing and sustainable teaching practices has been a challenge throughout my twenty-five-year teaching career.

With the arrival of my son in 2007, and over the next few years my three daughters, my priorities shifted dramatically. Coupled with the massive expansion of technology in the early 2000s and internet in the classroom, the complexity of teaching only grew as time went on. I didn't want my identity as a teacher to be primary. I instead wanted to be the best husband and father I could be. Still, I felt deeply compelled to serve my students to the best of my ability by helping them develop a love of learning so that they could unleash their full potential and grow as whole people.

The Wallace Family in 2015. My wife, Nikki, and our children: Will, Samantha, Norah and Izzy

Teaching brings incredible highs—those moments when a new idea catches fire in the classroom, when students light up with enthusiasm and engagement. But it also brings significant challenges: parents who offload responsibility for their kids onto teachers, districts that push countless initiatives that seem disconnected from classroom reality, and administrators whose actions contradict their stated values. Despite these challenges, I've never regretted choosing education as my profession. Working with young people, and helping to unleash their potential and creativity, remains a calling I deeply believe in.

I knew that giving my best to my classroom while balancing my commitments to my growing family would require a change in mindset and an increase in my skill set.

## The First Breakthrough: Getting Things Done

My quest to balance my life led me to take a deep dive into the world of productivity and time management. In 2008, my brother, Todd, introduced me to David Allen's Getting Things Done (GTD) methodology. The principles and practices I was learning and building into my life were countercultural yet so intuitive. I dove in headfirst to learn and apply all that I could.

The impact of the GTD methodology on my personal and professional life was profound. I was feeling calmer, less stressed, and more focused, all the while experiencing the most productive and fruitful season of my life. I started thinking, "What if I'd had these skills and tools earlier in life? Shouldn't I be passing these skills and tools on to the students I'm working with?" Unfortunately, at the time, there weren't any GTD resources available for students. So, I began writing, teaching, and designing lessons for my elementary classroom. This process eventually led to coauthoring *Getting Things Done for Teens*, which aims to equip young people with the essential executive function skills and learning behaviors

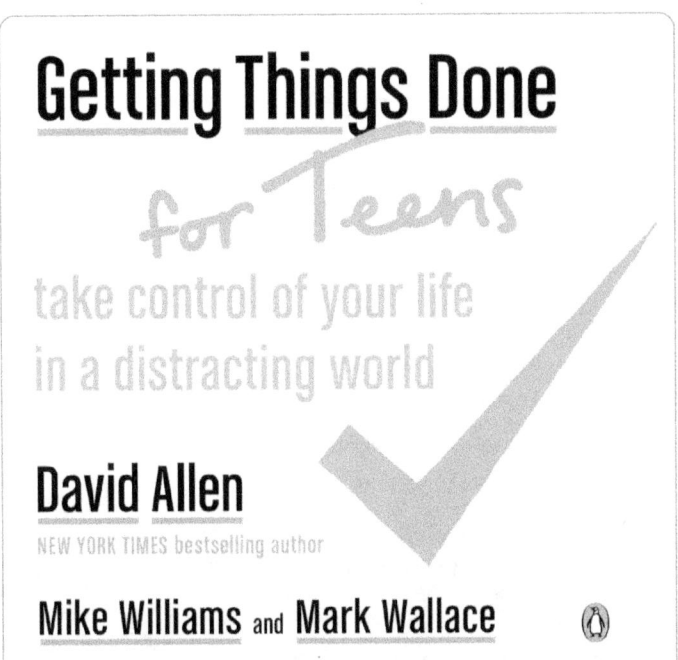

GTD for Teens was released in 2018.
Penguin Publishing Group

they need to thrive. Writing that book was among the most impactful work I've done in my life, and I continue to benefit from practicing and teaching GTD to this day.

## What GTD Alone Couldn't Solve

With elite productivity systems in place, my personal and professional life felt more balanced than ever. But I soon discovered that efficiency alone couldn't solve some of the deeper challenges of teaching. I learned to effectively manage my time and attention, yet I still spent hours creating lessons and projects. I had generated more margin in my schedule to plan creative lessons, yet student engagement still varied wildly. Some fundamental questions remained: How do we, as educators, maintain energy and enthusiasm for teaching amid ever-changing demands? How do we create authentic learning experiences for students without burning out?

Teaching in a multiage classroom meant I couldn't rely on recycled lesson plans or comfortable routines. With the same students for multiple years, I was forced to keep content fresh while adapting to new standards and maintaining high engagement. That need for novelty had always been a challenging balance that tested my creative capacity and the sustainability of my practice. I needed something more—not systems for managing my work but frameworks that transformed the work itself.

## The Second Breakthrough: EduProtocols

We all have had colleagues who push boundaries. The ones who seem to operate on education's fringes, constantly pushing the envelope. I have been blessed throughout my career to work with a variety of incredible teachers and innovators. In more recent years, however, that boundary-pushing colleague was Matt Gabrielson, who taught just a few rooms down the hall from me.

As I pondered how to continually adapt and refresh my own classroom practices, I'd hear Matt sharing these new frameworks he was using, which were transforming his teaching practice. I'd mention something I'd tried to teach and he'd say something along the lines of "Bro, you should just try a Cyber Sandwich." I'd hear him name these frameworks and explain what he would do, and unfortunately I'd just scratch my head and move on.

I'm now embarrassed to admit how long I ignored his excitement. I assumed EduProtocols were just another passing educational fad or a mere repackaging of cooperative protocols I was already using. After twenty-five years in public education, I had developed a healthy skepticism toward the endless parade of initiatives and "game-changing" methodologies that perpetually swept through our profession. But I'd like to think I've also learned to recognize legitimate innovation when I see it. And Matt's persistence—and more importantly, the visible transformation in his teaching energy—eventually broke through my resistance.

When I finally paid attention to what Matt was sharing, I asked some deeper questions and tried piloting a few of the EduProtocol frameworks he introduced me to: Thin Slides, Fast and Curious, and several others.

**Mark**

I spent years perfecting productivity systems to manage my teaching life, but the real game changer was designing learning experiences that actually energized me instead of draining me.

The first time I implemented Fast and Curious (a fast-paced vocabulary acquisition lesson framework) with my students, I was struck by how quickly they adapted to the format. By our third session, they needed minimal direction—they knew the framework and could focus entirely on the content. What would have previously taken me hours to prepare as individual lessons had just taken minutes, and student engagement was higher than ever.

This wasn't just efficiency—this was transformation.

My work with GTD helped me empower students with autonomy and agency, and now EduProtocols were maximizing engagement. I also noticed something I hadn't felt in a while—I was having fun. I was leaving school earlier, feeling more energized. These frameworks weren't draining my time and energy or taxing my systems; they were actually generating margin, or space, in my teaching practice—creating more opportunities to think, innovate, and engage more deeply with my students. EduProtocols provided structured creativity, allowing me to focus on content and connection rather than constantly reinventing my instructional methods.

## From User to Designer

EduProtocols aren't just for a select few innovative teachers—they represent a highly accessible approach any educator can embrace. Moreover, the frameworks yield multiple benefits: They provide structure while allowing for creativity, they create authentic feedback loops for students, and perhaps most importantly for me, they make teaching more sustainable by generating the extra time and thinking space we all need.

This manual grew out of my journey from EduProtocol skeptic to practitioner to designer. It's written for every teacher who believes in the power of innovation but needs practical, sustainable ways to implement it. Whether you're looking to refresh your practice, engage students more deeply, or find new energy in your teaching, the EduProtocol design process offers a path forward. In the following chapters, we'll explore how to create, iterate, and implement protocols that work for your specific teaching context.

My story isn't unique—it's the story of countless educators seeking better ways to serve their students while maintaining their own professional vitality. At twenty-five years in, when I was questioning whether to continue in education or pursue something else, EduProtocols opened a new chapter in my teaching journey.

## What's Ahead

In the chapters ahead, you'll discover practical frameworks for creating your own EduProtocols, starting with essential design principles and exploring how feedback loops power student engagement. You'll learn to transform traditional lesson structures into repeatable protocols that save time while deepening student learning. Whether you're brand-new to EduProtocols or ready to design your own, each chapter builds the specific skills you'll need to revolutionize your teaching practice without burning out.

This book is ultimately about shifting your perspective—moving from seeing yourself as a content deliverer to recognizing yourself as a learning experience designer. When teachers embrace their role as EduProtocol designers, they begin to see teaching challenges as design opportunities, and they develop the ability to recognize when something can be improved, simplified, or made more engaging. My hope is that this manual will help you discover the designer within yourself, creating EduProtocols that not only engage your students but also sustain your own passion for teaching.

On a broader scale, imagine thousands of educators designing and sharing innovative EduProtocols, creating a grassroots movement that transforms education from the classroom up. Every protocol you create has the potential to inspire teachers across the world, engaging students you'll never meet. Together, we can build a community where teachers support teachers through EduProtocols, where creativity replaces compliance, and where both students and educators thrive.

If you're ready to move beyond the status quo and design learning experiences that energize both you and your students, you're in the right place.

## Your Turn

Reflect on your own teaching journey. What teaching challenges have pushed you to innovate?

# Chapter 2
# The Deeper Messaging Behind Design

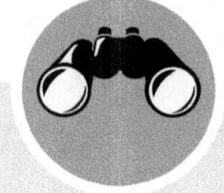

Before we dig any deeper into designing EduProtocols, let's take a broader look at design, especially as it relates to education.

## The Hidden Messages in Educational Design

In education, design has historically been treated as an afterthought—something to consider only after the "important" teaching decisions are made: lectures, lesson plans, assessments, data. Walk through any school building and you'll see the evidence of design's disregard: classroom walls cluttered with well-intentioned but overwhelming displays, worksheets that confuse more than they guide, presentation slides that either put students to sleep or bombard them with colors and animation. I've been guilty of all of these design failures.

Education often swings between design extremes. Some physical classrooms are sterile and understimulating, while others overflow with visual noise. The term *cells and bells* was coined for a reason. Have you ever walked into a classroom and immediately felt stressed, chaotic, or overstimulated? Or walked into a room and immediately groaned at how dull the environment makes you feel? Teachers are often either obsessed with filling space or at a loss for what to do with it.

Student materials and worksheets tell similar stories. Some micromanage every aspect of student response, while others provide so little structure that students struggle to understand expectations. Think about multiple-choice questions so prescriptive they eliminate student voice entirely or broad assignments like "write about your thoughts" that provide no scaffolding or direction. Whether we overcontrol through rigid formats or undersupport with vague prompts, we can unintentionally rob students of meaningful learning opportunities.

Our presentation slides frequently fall into similar traps of either dull karaoke—reading exactly what's on the screen—or chaotic design that obscures rather than clarifies learning. How many staff development sessions have you sat through where someone simply read what was on the screen while you wished they'd just emailed you the slide deck? Or sessions where the presenter tried to dress up mind-numbing or unorganized content by including a funny meme? How often do we as teachers fall into the same trap?

None of this is about pointing fingers or triggering guilt. These design choices likely come from very good intentions—trying to make learning more engaging, trying to provide clear structure, trying to capture student attention. But as we'll explore in this chapter, design isn't about decoration. Design in education should be about clear and intentional communication, authentic student engagement, and most importantly, creating space for student voice and ownership.

Imagine classrooms where every design choice—from wall displays to digital templates—amplifies student thinking rather than competing with it. Picture learning materials so intuitive that students immediately know what to do, freeing their cognitive energy for deep engagement with content rather than decoding instructions. When we get design right in education, we create environments where student creativity flourishes and teachers can focus on what matters most: facilitating powerful learning experiences.

## Font Choices: More than Aesthetics

What happens when we start to center design as an important, guiding principle of education? Consider something as simple as font choices. Is it possible that the fonts we, as educators, choose for our materials reflect something as deep as our teaching philosophy? Stay with me for a moment. For years, educators have grappled with making their materials appear more student-friendly, often focusing on appearance rather than on the underlying engagement of the activity itself.

Take Comic Sans. For the past twenty-five years, it's been elementary education's go-to font, adorning everything from worksheets to bulletin boards. Educators often gravitated toward it because it looked "kid-friendly" and "fun." But here's an uncomfortable truth: Making a worksheet *look* more fun doesn't automatically make it more engaging. Adding Comic Sans to a fill-in-the-blank vocabulary exercise is like putting a party hat on a filing cabinet—it doesn't change what's inside. Our goal shouldn't simply be to choose fonts that look kid-friendly; our goal should be to make design choices that bring out the best in our students.

Consider the typical worksheet. Decorative borders, multiple fonts, clip art in every corner—we've all seen them, maybe even created them. We choose "fun" decorations because, deep down, we know the activity itself isn't all that engaging. We add decorative elements to mask uninspiring content. It might look more appealing at first glance, but it doesn't improve the fundamental experience.

There's an even deeper, more troubling message in our design choices. In addition to overdesigning and decorating, there's a tendency to stifle and control student choice and output. So often we overmanage student materials and activities, creating elaborate templates that ask students to simply spit back information and fill in blanks. The hidden message here is this: "This is my information and creation, and your role is to conform, to fit into my plans." This isn't really about learning—it's about control and conformity. We inadvertently stifle student voice and creativity while missing opportunities to tap into something deeper.

This tendency toward controlling learning, rather than facilitating it, shows up even in how we approach fonts. For decades Times New Roman was the required standard for students to write their papers and complete their work. But why? Who decided this was to be the standard? Why did we start dictating font choices to students at all? Would it really be *that bad* if students used different fonts?

**Mark**

Decorative borders on worksheets are like laugh tracks on sitcoms—if you need them to signal "this is fun," maybe the content isn't actually fun. Kids see through artificial enthusiasm.

What if . . . instead of mandating specific fonts, we taught students about design principles and let them choose fonts that match the tone and goal of their work? When we create unnecessary constraints around formatting, we miss opportunities to empower student choice, creativity, and ultimately design literacy. For example, a student writing a serious research paper might choose Garamond for its clarity and professionalism, while another might select Courier for a creative writing piece to evoke a specific mood. These choices become part of the learning process itself.

The reality is that most teachers are caught in an impossible bind—they're required to cover predetermined curriculum standards within rigid timelines, often using mandated materials that weren't designed with engagement in mind. When you have thirty students, limited planning time, and pressure to prepare kids for standardized tests, it's far easier to add colorful borders to existing worksheets than to completely redesign learning experiences from scratch. Teachers aren't choosing boring activities because they lack creativity; they're often working within systems that prioritize coverage over engagement, compliance over innovation.

## Student Agency in Design

Design in education isn't about making everything minimalist or pretty, nor is it about abandoning structure and adopting chaos. Ultimately, everything we do in education needs to be about intentionality. We already have intentionality with the lessons we teach, the skills we elevate, the language we use with students. Why not have the same intentionality with the decor on the walls, the slides we project, the activities we push out to students? Our design choices reflect deeper, important questions.

Ask yourself the following:

- Who are you designing for? What captures their attention?
- What message does your design send about student ownership?

**Jon**

Mark isn't talking about "Pinterest classrooms" either. He is talking about a sense of balance, restraint, and clarity of design in our work.

- What is unnecessary in your design elements that might distract from learning?
- Where might you give design control back to your students?

Teachers Pay Teachers (TPT) offers thousands of visually appealing resources. But examine them through this lens: How many prioritize decoration over student agency? How many are designed to attract teacher-buyers rather than serve student-users? The issue extends beyond TPT to curriculum companies that package basic content in expensive, visually impressive materials that appeal to administrators but don't necessarily improve learning.

What if instead of catching the eyes of teachers and administrators, we focused on what students need, want, and find beneficial? What if we took a fresh look at how curricula are designed to see if they are working for the students rather than the teachers? What if the desires of the system became subservient to the learning needs and preferences of our students?

These questions point toward a fundamental shift from teachers as content controllers to teachers as learning experience facilitators. When students have agency in design choices, they develop critical thinking about visual communication, personal expression, and audience awareness. When materials are designed for actual use rather than visual appeal, learning becomes more accessible and authentic. Most importantly, when we design with students at the center, we create environments where their voices matter, their choices have impact, and their creativity drives learning forward.

**Marlena**

That super-simple, basic-looking EduProtocols template? It's not plain—it's powerful! Because it doesn't try to do the thinking for the student. The best templates aren't about showcasing how creative you are but about unleashing student creativity! Mark is going to show us how!

## EduProtocols Are About Intentional Design

EduProtocols, at their core, are frameworks. They are templates. (We will delve deeper into this in chapter 4). For now, the simple point here is that EduProtocols are strategically simplistic while richly complex in thinking. They are designed with the student at the forefront, not the teacher. They are designed to elevate content, student voice, and creativity. EduProtocols involve both learning and individuality. This is embedded deep within the EduProtocol DNA.

To bring it home, some of the most effective EduProtocol templates will at first glance appear bland. This isn't a design flaw—it's a feature. Clean, simple templates send a message: "This is a framework for *your* ideas, *your* creativity, *your* voice." EduProtocol design is intended to create space for student ownership and personalization. This is one aspect that sets EduProtocol design apart.

You could call this approach *productive minimalism*—stripping away everything that doesn't serve student thinking while maintaining just enough structure to support learning. Unlike traditional worksheets, EduProtocols deliberately step back to make room for student voice. The goal is to create frameworks so intuitive that students can focus entirely on content rather than figuring out what they're supposed to do. This approach requires tremendous restraint—resisting the urge to fill every space, control every response, or anticipate every possible student need through prescriptive design.

My hope in this chapter is not to discourage or embarrass anyone who uses worksheets or creates content for their students. Instead, my hope is that you are inspired to look more deeply at what engages and doesn't engage your students. You see, you already have what it takes to be an EduProtocol designer. Every time you've adapted a lesson to better serve your students, every time you've stripped away unnecessary complexity to focus on what matters—you've been designing. The key is learning to do it intentionally, with purpose and sensitivity to how design choices impact student engagement and ownership.

In the next chapter, we'll explore some fundamental principles of graphic design and their role in education. You'll discover how simple design choices can transform learning experiences and create more space for student voice. But remember—the goal isn't to create perfectly designed materials. Basic materials can still function as deep learning experiences that put students first if they are designed *intentionally*.

### Your Turn

Choose a recent learning activity you've created. Examine it through the lens of student agency: What messages does its design send about who owns the learning? Where might you strip away decoration to make room for student voice? How could you redesign one element to shift more ownership to students? This reflective practice is your first step toward intentional EduProtocol design.

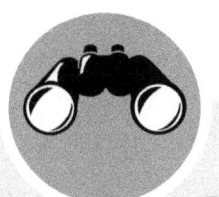

# Chapter 3
## Design Basics from a Layman Designer

**I'm not a professional designer.** So very, very far from it. For years, I kind of knew what I thought looked good and what I didn't like, but I couldn't really tell you why. I'd see other teachers' materials and think, "That works better than mine," but I couldn't pinpoint the reason. Then I married my wife, Nikki, a natural artist and musician, a professional graphic designer. Slowly, through hearing her talk and seeing her process, I began to understand some basics and put words to my own thoughts, and eventually I began transforming my own teaching materials.

The real breakthrough wasn't just learning design principles—it was realizing that good educational design isn't about making things look pretty. It's about making them work for students. Here's some of what I've learned along the way.

## Five Principles That Transform Teaching Materials

Five basic principles of design transformed my approach to teaching materials. These five principles will make your materials more effective for students and more sustainable for you. Students will navigate your resources intuitively, focusing their cognitive energy on learning rather than figuring out instructions. Meanwhile, you'll make design decisions with confidence rather than guesswork, creating materials that serve learning goals. The result is a classroom where design supports rather than competes with education.

# User Experience

## Definition

The intuitive flow and clarity of your materials that allows students to understand and navigate without explicit instruction.

## Why It Matters

When students don't have to figure out how to use a resource, they can focus entirely on learning the content. Poor user experience creates cognitive load that distracts from learning objectives.

## How to Implement

Students shouldn't need lengthy instructions for how to navigate materials. Keep things simple and commonsense. We read left to right, top to bottom. Design with this natural flow in mind. Use visual cues like arrows, numbers, or highlighted elements to guide attention.

The best-designed learning materials create what designers call a *natural user experience*—students instinctively know where to look, what to do, and how to navigate through the content. Before sharing materials with students, ask yourself, "Would a new student know what to do with this without explanation?" If not, the design might need rethinking.

## Common Pitfall

Assuming students will "figure it out" or providing lengthy written directions instead of creating an intuitive design. If you need extensive instructions for using the material, the design likely needs simplification.

**Marlena**

Don't design for applause; design for access. Fancy doesn't equal functional. If students are lost in the layout, they are not learning the content. (The downfall of almost every worksheet ever made!) Clean, obvious, and intuitive wins every time.

## Balance

### Definition

The distribution of visual weight across your materials, creating stability and directing attention.

### Why It Matters

Balanced designs feel ordered and comfortable. They help students focus on content rather than being unconsciously distracted by lopsided layouts.

### How to Implement

Think of your slides or materials like a seesaw. When you place a heavy element (large image, dark color, bold text) on one side, balance it with something on the other side. Step back and scan your design: Does it feel tilted or stable? Where does your eye naturally go first?

### Common Pitfall

Creating top-heavy designs or clustering all important elements on one side, leaving students unsure where to focus their attention.

## Alignment

### Definition

The consistent positioning of elements along invisible lines or grids.

### Why It Matters

Nothing says "this is thrown together" like misaligned elements. Whether we are consciously aware or not, there exists visual order and visual chaos. There are students in your classroom who are

**Jon**

Readability guru Steve Krug has three main rules to maximize readability. My favorite is "make everything in text as short as possible, then cut it in half." Brevity = faster uptake by the brain.

> **Mark**
> 
> "Close-enough" alignment is like being "almost" on key—everyone notices, even if they can't explain why something feels off. Precision in small details builds trust in big ideas.

perpetually seeking to make order out of what feels like chaos. Alignment is simple but means more than you might think!

## How to Implement

Use your software's alignment tools and guides. In Google Slides, turn on guides (View → Guides) to help align elements. Line up text, images, and other elements along the same invisible lines rather than placing them randomly.

When text and images line up:

- Materials look more thoughtful, intentional, and professional.
- Information flows better.
- Students focus on content instead of chaos.

## Common Pitfall

"Close-enough" alignment that looks haphazard. Even small misalignments can create a subconscious impression of disorder or carelessness. Technology makes alignment easy, so make the most of it!

# Color

## Definition

A powerful communication tool that guides attention, creates meaning, and establishes visual hierarchy.

Color is *not* decoration—it's communication. Colors matter. Confession: I don't know color. Have *you* ever stopped to think about why exit signs and stop signs are red? I was embarrassingly far into my career before I was made aware of the fact that red draws the eye first. What else didn't I know about color?!

## Why It Matters

Color influences attention, mood, and information processing. Strategic color use helps students identify patterns and prioritize information.

## How to Implement

Choose a limited color palette (three to five colors) from a tool like coolors.co, or pick a preferred color and ask your favorite AI tool for complementary colors. Develop your palette, and then use it consistently. Assign meaning to colors (e.g., blue for examples, orange for key terms) and maintain this system across materials. Save hex codes of your chosen colors for easy reference and consistency across digital and print and across your lesson slides and class website.

**COLORS**

Scan the QR Code to see the full palette in color

This is the color pallette and hex values used for every EduProtocol design in this book.

## Common Pitfall

Using decorative colors without purpose or using too many colors creates visual noise. Remember that bright colors don't make a boring, stale activity engaging.

# Empty Space

## Definition

The intentional use of unfilled areas in your design (also called *white space* or *negative space*).

> **Jon**
> Try using a condensed font on your student materials. It gets more text in less space while being clear and readable. My favorite is Barlow Condensed.

> **Marlena**
> Let the eye rest. We don't want our student work to have a "Where's Waldo" effect.

### Why It Matters

Empty space gives visual breathing room that helps students focus on what matters. Cluttered materials overwhelm and confuse learners.

### How to Implement

Start with a blank canvas and add only what's necessary. Give important elements room to stand out by surrounding them with empty space. When in doubt, leave it out.

### Common Pitfall

Feeling compelled to fill every available space, creating cluttered, overwhelming materials that diffuse student attention instead of focusing it.

## Summary: Minimal Design, Maximum Learning

Your design shouldn't compete with student thinking. Keep things simple:

- Use consistent alignment.
- Limit fonts and colors.
- Include only essential elements.
- Leave room for student personalization.

As discussed in chapter 2, the best EduProtocols will provide structure without constraint. They will *guide* learning while leaving space for creativity and personal expression.

Take the Thin Slides EduProtocol, for instance. This template demonstrates restraint at its most powerful—a single blank slide. Students may add only two elements: one image and one word. No decorative borders, no extensive directions, no elaborate formatting options. This apparent simplicity is strategically designed. The abundant white space forces students to be selective about their content, while the single-image requirement pushes them toward visual thinking. The clean layout ensures their ideas, not the template design, capture attention. Students immediately understand the constraints and can focus their energy on crafting a compelling message rather than navigating complex formatting requirements.

We can embrace that design philosophy throughout our teaching materials too. Think of design like a good referee—it should support the game without becoming the center of attention. When design works well, students focus on content rather than figuring out layout.

In the next chapter, we'll look at how these principles come together in creating EduProtocols. For now, remember that good design isn't about rules or beauty—it's about making learning accessible for your students.

## Your Turn

Before moving on, consider these questions: What's one design element in your teaching materials that might be competing with rather than supporting student learning? How might you simplify it using the principles we've discussed?

# Chapter 4
## What Makes an EduProtocol an EduProtocol?

**Throughout the previous chapters, we've explored how traditional educational materials often create barriers between students and learning—through cluttered design, overcontrolling templates, and activities that prioritize compliance over creativity.** EduProtocols represent a fundamental shift away from these practices. They streamline teaching while deepening engagement, reduce prep time while increasing authentic learning, and create sustainable practices that energize both teachers and students. Most importantly, they transform classrooms from spaces of passive consumption into communities of active creation and collaboration.

The design philosophy behind EduProtocols centers on strategic simplicity—creating frameworks that are sophisticated in their educational impact yet elegant in their execution. Every element serves learning rather than decoration, every constraint empowers rather than restricts, and every repetition builds mastery rather than boredom. EduProtocols operate on the principle that when design gets out of the way, learning takes center stage. They're built to fade into the background once students understand the framework, allowing cognitive energy to flow toward content mastery, creative expression, and meaningful collaboration rather than figuring out what to do next.

Given this design philosophy, what are the essential characteristics that distinguish EduProtocols from traditional teaching activities?

## Defining by What It's Not

In education, sometimes we define new concepts by explaining what the concepts are not. It's an approach that helps clear misconceptions before building new understanding. So let's start there.

An EduProtocol is *not*:

- A stand-alone slide or worksheet to be completed and forgotten.
- A single-use activity that serves one learning objective.
- An isolated task completed in silence.
- A traditional assignment repackaged with fancy fonts.
- A tech tool that prioritizes flash over function.
- A one-size-fits-all template that constrains student thinking.
- A collection of busywork disguised as innovation.
- An activity done without feedback or peer interaction.

So, what makes an EduProtocol an EduProtocol? EduProtocols are frameworks that transform how students engage with content across subjects and over time. They are carefully designed learning experiences that grow with your students, adapt to different content areas, and create authentic opportunities for engagement and feedback.

Broadly, then, an EduProtocol *is*:

- A repeatable framework that works across multiple content areas and subjects.
- A collaborative learning experience that incorporates peer feedback and discussion.
- A structured yet flexible template that empowers student voice and creativity.

> **Marlena**
>
> Slapping a cute font on an overly structured slide (a.k.a. worksheet) doesn't make it an EduProtocol. The magic is in the structure: simple, clear, repeatable.

> **Jon**
>
> And don't get me started on unneeded borders. =)

- An engaging activity that connects to youth culture while maintaining academic rigor.
- A multi-standard learning opportunity that integrates eight to twelve educational objectives.
- A confidence-building experience that starts simple and grows in complexity.
- A time-efficient teaching tool that reduces prep while increasing engagement.
- A feedback-rich environment that provides immediate responses from multiple sources.

## The Four Cs in Action

Communication, creativity, critical thinking, and collaboration aren't just buzzwords in an EduProtocol—they're built into its DNA. Known collectively as *twenty-first-century skills*, the Four Cs represent the essential competencies students need for success in school, work, and life. Rather than teaching these skills in isolation, EduProtocols weave them together naturally, creating learning experiences where students practice all four simultaneously.

Students aren't just consuming content. Here's what they're doing instead:

- Discussing ideas with peers
- Creating original content
- Analyzing and evaluating information
- Working together toward common goals

Take the 8 pARTS EduProtocol as an example. Students collaborate to identify parts of speech from a shared image, think critically about word functions and relationships, communicate their findings to classmates, and create original sentences using their discoveries. All four skills happen organically within a single framework.

This integrated approach mirrors real-world problem-solving, where communication, creativity, critical thinking, and collaboration work together rather than in isolation. Students develop these essential skills without the artificial separation that often makes them feel disconnected from actual learning.

## Multiple Standards, One Framework

A solid EduProtocol weaves together around eight to twelve educational standards into a cohesive experience. These standards aren't forced together—they flow naturally through the process. You might have the following:

- Reading and analysis
- Digital literacy
- Communication skills
- Creative expression
- Critical thinking

And they're all working together in service of learning.

Consider the StoryScan EduProtocol (you'll read about this in chapter 7). Students analyze fiction elements while creating emoji plot summaries and rating books with evidence-based justification. This single framework integrates reading comprehension, literary analysis, digital communication, creative expression, critical evaluation, and presentation skills. Students master multiple standards simultaneously rather than learning them in isolation.

This approach maximizes instructional time while helping students see how skills connect in real-world applications. Instead of spending separate days on character analysis, plot summary, and opinion writing, students develop all these competencies together, creating a deeper understanding of how academic skills work in practice.

## Ease of Integration

EduProtocols aren't isolated experiences. They integrate with the following:

- Multiple subject areas

- Different learning styles
- Various tech tools
- Diverse student populations

This flexibility makes them powerful tools for any classroom.

Think of an EduProtocol like a well-designed game controller—it should feel natural in students' hands, be intuitive to use, and work across multiple platforms. The best ones become invisible, letting students focus entirely on learning.

The Fast and Curious EduProtocol demonstrates this versatility perfectly. Whether students are learning vocabulary in English, exploring scientific terms in biology, or mastering historical concepts in social studies, the same framework applies. This adaptability means teachers don't need different strategies for different subjects or student needs. One well-designed framework serves multiple purposes, reducing cognitive load for both teachers and students while maintaining engagement across diverse learning contexts. Students transfer their familiarity with the protocol from one subject to another, accelerating their comfort and success.

## Feedback Loops That Matter

Immediate feedback is crucial, but it doesn't always have to come from the teacher. EduProtocols incorporate multiple feedback channels:

- Peer discussion and review
- Whole-class sharing
- Digital interactions
- Youth culture elements (likes, comments, reactions)
- Teacher guidance
- AI guidance and coaching

These feedback loops aren't just about assessment—they're about engagement and growth. They create continuous cycles where students receive immediate responses to their thinking,

---

**Marlena**

The magic of a great EduProtocol? It fades into the background. When the design disappears, learning takes center stage.

allowing them to adjust, improve, and engage more deeply in real time.

In the Thin Slides EduProtocol, feedback happens instantly and continuously. Students create their one-word, one-image slides, then every student briefly shares the thinking process behind their choices. Peers immediately react with questions, connections, or interpretations. The entire process lasts only minutes, but every voice is heard and multiple feedback channels are activated.

## The Sizzle Factor

Here's where many educational frameworks fall short—they forget that learning often needs some spark. EduProtocols embrace youth culture without sacrificing substance. This connection to student interests creates familiar entry points that make academic content more accessible and engaging.

This might mean any of the following:

- Playful, memorable EduProtocol names
- Contemporary feedback loops
- Multiple ways to interact
- Authentic connections to student interests
- Choice

For example: When students create a Thin Slide, they're engaging with the same visual communication principles that drive successful TikTok and Instagram content—concise messaging, visual impact, and personal voice—all while processing academic content.

This isn't about false hype. *It's about making learning relevant and engaging while maintaining authenticity.*

The sizzle factor works because it meets students where they are rather than demanding they adapt to outdated formats. When learning feels familiar and relevant, students engage more deeply with challenging content. They're not just tolerating academic work—they're seeing connections between their interests and meaningful learning, which builds intrinsic motivation that extends far beyond individual assignments.

## Smart Start: Building Confidence

Every EduProtocol begins with a Smart Start—an introduction to the framework with low-stakes, fun, kid-friendly content. This isn't dumbing things down; it's strategic. When cognitive load on content is low, students can master the protocol itself. They take in the design, explore the user experience, and find where their voice fits. Once they've got the framework down, you can gradually increase the complexity of the content. It's like learning to juggle—you might start with scarves before moving to balls, then clubs.

## The Power of Repetition

EduProtocols are meant to be used again and again, across different subjects and content areas. This repetition isn't redundant—it's revolutionary. When students master the framework, they can focus mental energy on content rather than figuring out directions. It's like driving a car: Once you master the basic operations, you can concentrate on where you're going rather than relearning how to drive.

Consider how the 8 pARTS EduProtocol works across an entire school year. In September, students might analyze parts of speech using a funny meme meant to generate laughs and build classroom community. By October, they're using the same framework to examine a historical speech. In January, they apply it to a scientific article about ecosystems. Each time, the protocol structure remains constant while the content grows more sophisticated. Students transfer their mastery of the framework from literature to history to science, building confidence and competence with each repetition.

This approach creates cognitive efficiency that traditional teaching methods rarely achieve. Instead of spending mental energy learning new procedures for each lesson, students can

> **Mark**
> Smart Starts aren't about dumbing things down—they're about building confidence. It's the difference between throwing kids in the deep end and teaching them to love the water first.

dive immediately into deep thinking about content. The familiar framework becomes a mental scaffold that supports increasingly complex learning. Students develop automaticity with the process, freeing their minds to engage with challenging ideas and make connections across disciplines.

## Essential Principles for Success

Understanding what makes an EduProtocol effective is one thing; implementing it successfully in real classrooms is another. Many teachers worry about losing control when they shift from traditional, highly structured activities to frameworks that invite student voice and creativity. Others fear that the open-ended nature of EduProtocols might lead to chaos, off-task behavior, or students who "don't get it." These concerns are understandable—most of us were trained in educational approaches that prioritize predictability and compliance over creativity and collaboration.

Successful EduProtocol implementation requires a fundamental shift in how we define teaching success. Instead of measuring success by how quietly students work or how precisely they follow directions, we begin to value engagement, authentic thinking, and creative problem-solving. This doesn't mean abandoning structure or expectations; it means creating frameworks that support rather than constrain student learning. The following principles help teachers navigate this transition while creating the conditions for students using EduProtocols to thrive.

## Safety First

Creating a safe space for creativity and expression isn't optional—it's foundational. When we invite student voice and creativity, we are asking students to be vulnerable. Students need to know they can take creative risks without fear of judgment or ridicule. Smart Starts play a crucial role here, establishing not just the EduProtocol but the culture of support and acceptance that makes innovation possible.

**Mark**

If you want kids to take risks in their thinking, they have to feel safe to take risks in their design.

## The Strategic Use of Time

"I'm done, what do I do now?" If you smiled reading that, you're not alone. It's the eternal question that has echoed through classrooms since the beginning of education. But here's where EduProtocols are different—they regularly use defined time limits strategically. Sometimes *done* means completion of the task, and other times it can just mean that time is up!

Timers in EduProtocols aren't just about classroom management; they become about equity and psychological safety. They can:

- Prevent early finishers from disengaging.
- Keep perfectionists from overthinking.
- Create a shared external challenge (time) rather than internal pressure.
- Level the playing field for diverse learners.
- Provide natural transitions and closure.

I've found this especially powerful for students dealing with the complexities of the autism spectrum, who often benefit from clear time boundaries and expectations. With practice, the timer becomes an objective guide rather than a subjective pressure.

## Embracing Creative Chaos

When you invite student voice and creativity, someone will inevitably color outside the lines. They'll take your carefully designed EduProtocol and do something completely unexpected with it. And that's okay.

Don't get discouraged when:

- A student interprets the task differently than intended.
- The first run-through is messy—it's just the first try.
- Creative expressions vary widely.
- Some students push boundaries.

Remember:

- Clear objectives matter more than rigid compliance.

- Authentic feedback guides improvement.
- Modeling shows possibilities without limiting creativity.
- Repetition builds understanding.
- Each iteration gets better.

The beauty of EduProtocols lies not in perfect execution but in creating spaces where students can explore, create, and grow—safely, strategically, and sometimes surprisingly.

## Moving Forward

The attributes we've explored—from the integration of the Four Cs to the power of repetition—work together to create learning experiences that are fundamentally different from traditional classroom activities. EduProtocols transform teaching from a series of isolated assignments into a coherent framework for building student capacity, confidence, and creativity.

When I first started implementing EduProtocols, I was struck by how different my classroom felt during these activities compared with traditional lessons. Students leaned in rather than checked out. They built on each other's ideas rather than working in isolation. The energy was palpable—not the frantic energy of entertainment but the focused energy of minds truly engaged in meaningful work. These weren't just better activities; they were glimpses of what education could look like when design serves learning rather than control.

In the next chapter, I'll walk you through my own process of creating EduProtocols from initial concept to classroom implementation. You might be surprised by how many elements of a great protocol you already have in your teaching repertoire.

You've likely already created learning frameworks that contain many EduProtocol elements.

**Jon**

In sports, coaches know teams grow the most in an entire season between the first and second game. Why? They've seen a real opponent. In school, we try to get to the second or third rep quickly, without belaboring the early awkward attempts, so we can get to the "good ones."

**Mark**

The creative-chaos phase of EduProtocols can feel terrifying to high-control teachers. But chaos isn't the opposite of learning—boredom is. Sometimes messiness means thinking is happening.

## Your Turn

Inventory your teaching repertoire for activities that already contain EduProtocol elements. Which ones include feedback loops? Which incorporate student creativity? Which are repeatable with different content? Identify one promising activity and list two to three modifications that might transform it into a true EduProtocol. Remember, you've likely already created frameworks that are just steps away from becoming powerful EduProtocols.

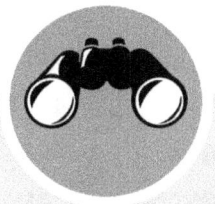

# Chapter 5
## The Process of EduProtocol Design

**My journey from using EduProtocols to designing EduProtocols didn't start with a lightning bolt of inspiration.** It started with failure—or what felt like it at the time.

### Seeing Through New Eyes

When I first discovered EduProtocols, I started seeing my teaching practice through refreshed eyes. Early on in my career, I was introduced to Eric Jensen's brain-compatible learning elements. His research identified specific conditions that optimize how the brain learns—elements like emotional engagement, meaningful patterns, choice, movement, social interaction, and immediate feedback.

These weren't new concepts to most teachers, but Jensen's work helped educators understand why certain teaching practices consistently worked while others fell flat. His brain-compatible elements provided a scientific framework for what many teachers intuitively knew: Learning happens best when students feel safe, engaged, and connected to both content and community.

While I had known about brain-compatible learning elements my entire career, they integrated effortlessly when I was applying EduProtocols, coming to life in new ways and making even more sense. EduProtocols naturally align with how the brain learns best: multiple repetitions leading to mastery, emotional connection and safety, social interaction and immediate feedback, and relevance and

Based on Eric Jensen's book "Teaching With the Brain in Mind"

patternmaking. They also connect seamlessly with education researcher Robert Marzano's work on engagement and effective instruction, which identified teaching strategies that work best when students actively participate in learning.

But for me, the real revelation wasn't about educational theory. It was directly tied to what I valued most philosophically, which was my positioning as an educator—where I stood in relation to my students, both literally and figuratively.

## Shoulder to Shoulder, Not Toe to Toe

Traditional teaching so often puts us toe to toe with students, in the role of authoritarian knowledge-dispenser. EduProtocols helped me to maintain and even build on the shoulder-to-shoulder position, what current education-speak refers to as the *warm demander* stance. This positioning allowed me to hold high expectations but to express them through coaching rather than commanding, guiding rather than directing.

At this point in my growing use of EduProtocols, it had become apparent that I was going all in.

While EduProtocols had transformed my classroom experience, I quickly discovered they weren't perfect. I found that even the most thoughtfully designed protocols could potentially benefit from some visual refinement and adaptation. In addition, as I looked across my curriculum, I realized that no existing collection of EduProtocols was going to address every unique teaching challenge I faced. This chapter chronicles both aspects of my design journey: The first was learning to thoughtfully redesign existing EduProtocols to better serve my students through improved visual consistency and user experience. The second was to eventually develop the skills to create entirely new EduProtocols when existing options didn't meet my specific learning objectives. Both processes taught me that effective EduProtocol design isn't about following a formula—it's about understanding the underlying principles that make learning frameworks successful, then applying those prin-

---

**Mark**

"Shoulder to shoulder, not toe to toe" became a teaching mantra. When you're fighting students, you've already lost. When you're coaching them, everyone wins.

**Marlena**

Why visual continuity matters: Students, like adults, benefit from visual anchors. When your templates use a consistent design language (naming, icons, colors, layout), you lower cognitive load. This allows students to focus on the content instead of figuring out the process. We've tried to do this with the EduProtocol templates that we make, but you can do this at the classroom level even more!

ciples through intentional choices that prioritize student engagement and authentic learning.

## Seeing a Need: Icons That Sizzle

As I grew my repertoire of EduProtocols, I was looking online for more and more visuals and templates. I was noticing that many of the designs of the EduProtocol icons and templates were visually inconsistent. This wasn't a design flaw, necessarily; it was a natural result of a vast community of educators all openly sharing what they had created and used. This generosity of the EduProtocol community was actually one of the things I fell in love with.

Taking what I had learned about visual design, I tweaked each of the EduProtocols I introduced to my students to make them part of our classroom "visual brand." This redesign process was not about ego or personalization; it was about continuity. I knew the recognition of color and pattern would help some of my students. And because I had come to enjoy learning about and playing with design, I moved from tweaking to remaking icons and templates. As a result of being so hands-on with design, unpacking and repackaging the icons and templates, my understanding, buy-in, and enthusiasm for EduProtocols grew.

Before I knew it, I had created about two dozen EduProtocol icons, all based on my understanding of elements of design—visual continuity, color, alignment, use of space, etc. On a whim, I randomly shared

**Jon**

The consistent, clean, and fun logos Mark sent to my LinkedIn inbox for *our* work sold me on his vision and skills in about two seconds. The power of visuals!

This message thread in LinkedIn started this entire journey.

these new designs with Jon Corippo through social media. Jon responded, and our unexpected partnership began.

## The Next Challenge: Streamlining and Simplifying Current EduProtocol Templates

Many of the templates I found online were extremely helpful. However, because each iterator had added their own design choices, they were often inconsistent. My growing hope was that I could remake those templates with some visual continuity to match the new icons. I began stripping the EduProtocol templates down, trying to find ways to simplify and visually tie them together. Through the design process, I was also learning to ask myself better questions:

- Will this be visually recognizable to my students? (Color palette, fonts, patterns, etc.)
- Does it follow a commonsense visual order? (Left to right, top to bottom, etc.)
- What could I remove to reduce noise?
- What might I add that would naturally indicate what to do? (Colors, headers, arrows, etc.)
- Do the spaces for content invite student voice and offer choice?

Through redesigning existing EduProtocol icons and templates, I was deeply thinking about the user experience for my students. I can't underestimate how much this helped me understand EduProtocols.

## Moving from EduProtocol User to EduProtocol Designer

I was now feeling grounded using established protocols like 8 pARTS, Sentence pARTS, Thin Slides, Thick Slides, and Boo-

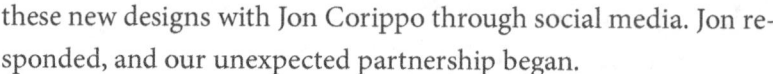

**Mark**

Don't underestimate the value of personalizing existing protocols. When you adapt them to your classroom's visual identity, you deepen both your understanding and your students' connection to the frameworks.

kaKucha in my classroom. Their effectiveness through repetition was eye-opening. (Kids learn and grow confident by trying something more than once? Who knew!) With reps, students knew what to expect with each protocol, and this meant we could focus entirely on content rather than constantly learning new procedures. Whether we were studying literature, history, or science, these frameworks adapted seamlessly. Perhaps most surprisingly, I found myself leaving school earlier, spending less time on prep and more time contemplating deeper learning connections.

This got me thinking: Where else in my teaching could I apply this approach?

As I continually looked at the content I was teaching and how I might incorporate the EduProtocols I was learning, I began to recognize the areas where I was teaching multiple standards separately. EduProtocol thinking has shown me that it's often better to teach standards together. As I was looking at morphology, biographies, or figurative language, I'd scan the EduProtocol books and EduProtocols Plus and scour the internet to see if a protocol already existed. When I couldn't find exactly what I needed, a fresh thought emerged: What was stopping me from creating my own?

And then . . . everything came together quickly and easily. I made countless EduProtocols that worked seamlessly, made all students happy, and changed the course of my life and lives around me forever.

Okay, it was not *at all* like that.

My first attempts weren't good. Initial designs were essentially worksheets or one-off activities with limited feedback loops. However, I couldn't shake the desire to get better at it. I kept looking at established EduProtocols and then at what I was making. I kept trying iterations with students, seeing where they were engaging, where they were confused, and what they were learning. I realized that I needed to get away from designing an "activity" for kids and get into designing a thinking framework. With some mentoring from Jon Corippo, I began to understand that EduProtocols aren't just a teaching technique for content; they're a pedagogical

> **Jon**
> True story: I used 8 pARTS (the original EP) for three school years before I realized that this kind of lesson could be replicated and adapted to other educational needs. Give yourself grace. This is a process, not an event.

mindset. Once I grasped this fundamental truth, my approach to designing my own transformed.

In chapters 6 to 13, I'll share my design journey with eight new EduProtocols, including both the successes and the stumbles. Because here's what I've learned: Developing the EduProtocol mindset comes first, and the design skill set follows. Once you start seeing your teaching through this lens, you'll likely discover countless opportunities to create powerful learning experiences for your students.

It is my belief that there are hundreds, even thousands, of EduProtocols already out there, buried in the minds and hearts of educators who are trying to find a better way to reach their students. What if we unearthed these original ideas and shared them with each other? What impact could we make on our teaching practice? On our student engagement?

Do you have an original EduProtocol hiding in you to share with the world? I believe you do.

## Starting the Design Journey

My journey from user to designer followed a winding path—from implementing existing protocols to redesigning icons, creating templates, and finally developing original frameworks. Your path might look different.

As you consider the possibility of designing your own EduProtocol, I encourage you to start here:

1. Look at your content through the lens of combination. Where can standards naturally flow together? Which skills complement each other? I found that reading standards often paired beautifully with writing and speaking skills.
2. Consider student output. How could students demonstrate learning in ways that:
    a. Can be repeated with different content.
    b. Tap into youth culture.
    c. Allow for creativity.

        d. Create natural feedback loops.
3. Start simple. Whether digital or analog, strip away everything that isn't essential. Remember: Students should be the content curators, not passive receivers.

## The First Try

Your first attempts won't be perfect. Mine certainly never are. Start with an idea and try a Smart Start—low-stakes content, clear time frame. Make it light and fun. Observe what happens:

- What engaged students?
- Where did they get stuck or have questions?
- Which feedback loops worked naturally? Where else could they be added?
- What unexpected creativity emerged?

## The Art of Iteration

When the first attempt doesn't go as planned, it's easy to give up. But this is where the real design work begins.

After each iteration:

- Adjust timings.
- Clarify instructions.
- Enhance feedback loops.
- Build in more student voice.
- Strip away what isn't working.

Remember, every "failed" attempt is valuable data and holds opportunity.

## Building in Feedback

Feedback isn't about assessment (although some feedback can replace traditional assessment). It's more about authentic engagement and building a community of learning and growth. Look for opportunities to build in the following:

- Peer responses
- Group discussions
- Digital interactions
- Teacher coaching moments
- Student self-reflection
- AI coaching

## Flippity for the Win

If you don't yet have a clear or established feedback loop for your design, just get kids talking.

However, speaking as a lifelong introvert, and a teacher who has watched kids struggle with introversion for twenty-five years, I want to urge you to never, *ever* tell kids to "find a partner." If I could ban one practice from all of education, it would be "find a partner." It isn't safe for all kids and can immediately create an awkward and hierarchical group dynamic. If this doesn't resonate with you, that's okay. You probably don't get it. You will have to trust me. It's a lazy and careless practice and is easily modified with an incredibly small amount of intentionality.

Need an alternative? Set up a free Flippity account and take three minutes to enter your class names, then randomize partners and groups all day long.

Pull Popsicle sticks, line kids up, count off and pair up . . . I don't care. Just permanently eliminate "find a partner."

Community gets built when everyone feels safe and included, when everyone interacts with all members. Emotional safety is a precursor to successfully integrating EduProtocols.

## The Power of Examples

Nothing teaches like student examples. When a student creates something particularly effective or unique, showcase it. Not as the

> **Jon**
> If kids are handing in something to wait for a grade, that's not an EduProtocol.

"right" way but as one possibility among many. These become part of your EduProtocol's evolution. Because you will be doing many repetitions, planting seeds for how to improve is an effective way of assuring students that they can.

It's just like an athlete watching game film. Watch yourself, watch others. Incorporate the best of other classmates, and eliminate content that is not effective.

## Grace, Space, and Pace

Give yourself permission to:

- Try things that might not work.
- Adjust on the fly.
- Learn alongside your students.
- Take time to refine and reflect.
- Celebrate small successes.

**Jon**

I love showing completed examples *before* we do an EduProtocol. It raises the bar immediately, and kids get up to speed with fewer reps.

In the next eight chapters, I'll share a few of the new EduProtocols I've designed, but more importantly, I'll share the messy, beautiful process of their creation. Some worked exactly as intended. Others took unexpected turns. All of them continue to illustrate something valuable about teaching and learning.

Remember, the goal isn't perfection. The goal is engagement, voice, and growth—for both you and your students.

### Your Turn

Identify a teaching challenge where you're currently using separate activities to address related standards. Sketch a simple framework that might bring these standards together in a repeatable format. Don't worry about perfection—just explore possibilities. What feedback loops might you incorporate? How could you make this framework adaptable across different content? The journey from idea to EduProtocol begins with this kind of exploratory thinking.

# SECTION 2
## 8 New EduProtocols and Their Iterative Origin Stories

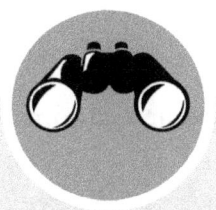

# Chapter 6
## Capitalization pARTS EduProtocol

This slide deck includes Capitalization pARTS recipe cards, templates, Smart Starts and student samples.

Capitalization pARTS transforms the teaching of capitalization rules from isolated grammar instruction into an engaging, repeatable framework that helps students internalize proper capitalization through consistent practice and visual reinforcement. This protocol builds on the familiar 8 pARTS family structure—where students identify all eight parts of speech within a single visual context—to create a fresh approach to one of the most fundamental yet persistently challenging aspects of writing.

## Design Story

Sometimes EduProtocols can emerge from the most basic classroom needs. While reviewing my students' writing samples, I noticed the same persistent pattern that has plagued humanity since the dawn of time: They weren't capitalizing. Some would capitalize random words for emphasis, others would write entire paragraphs without a single capital letter, and most were particularly inconsistent with proper nouns and titles.

The challenge wasn't that they hadn't been taught capitalization rules—they had, repeatedly, year after year. The issue was that this knowledge (or application) wasn't transferring to their actual writing. Traditional worksheets and isolated grammar lessons weren't creating the automaticity needed for consistent application.

I realized this was the perfect opportunity to apply an EduProtocol framework to address a fundamental writing skill. Looking at state standards, I identified the

**Jon**

His kids had been taught, but it wasn't sticking. Why? Most likely, too few reps, out of context, and with slow or no feedback.

**Mark**

My first EduProtocol felt like learning to parallel park—lots of adjustments, some frustration, but once you get it, you wonder why it seemed so hard.

six essential capitalization rules that students needed to master. Rather than teaching these rules in isolation, I wondered if combining them into a cohesive protocol might help students see capitalization as an integrated system rather than a collection of separate rules.

This was my first dive into designing an EduProtocol.

## Design Iterations

The first version of Capitalization pARTS was straightforward: six rules with blank spaces for students to write examples of each. While this was more organized than traditional worksheets, it still lacked the engagement factor and meaningful feedback loops that make EduProtocols effective.

I added space for an image that could serve as a prompt for practice. This visual element created a context for applying the rules, making the activity feel more purposeful. For example, using an image of a national park would naturally prompt students to apply rules about capitalizing place names, while a holiday scene would activate rules about capitalizing dates and special events.

---

RULE #1: Capitalize the beginning of a sentence.
He is dancing around in the endzone.

RULE #2: Capitalize the names of people and pets and titles of respect.
Justin Jefferson just scored a touchdown.

RULE #3: Capitalize days, months, and holidays.
The Vikings didn't have to play a game on Christmas Day.

RULE #4: Capitalize the names of places and geographic features.
They are playing in U.S. Bank Stadium.

RULE #5: Capitalize the names of historical events, periods, and documents.
The Vikings did not win the Super Bowl last year.

RULE #6: Capitalize proper adjectives, nationalities, and languages.
Justin Jefferson speaks English.

NAME: Veda

Capitalization pARTS Smart Start Student Sample

However, I noticed that some students still struggled with generating appropriate examples based solely on the image. Part of this was that it was difficult to extrapolate appropriate examples of all the capitalization rules with some images.

**RULE #1: Capitalize the beginning of a sentence.**
That guy is Martin Luther King Jr.

**RULE #2: Capitalize the names of people and pets and titles of respect.**
Martin Luther King Jr's famous phrase is "I have a dream."

**RULE #3: Capitalize days, months, and holidays.**
This picture was taken on August 28, 1963.

**RULE #4: Capitalize the names of places and geographic features.**
This was at the Lincoln Memorial, Washington D.C.

**RULE #5: Capitalize the names of historical events, periods, and documents.**
This was the March on Washington for Jobs and Freedom.

**RULE #6: Capitalize proper adjectives, nationalities, and languages.**
Martin Luther King Jr spoke English.

- **Date:** August 28, 1963
- **Event:** March on Washington for Jobs and Freedom
- **Location:** Lincoln Memorial, Washington D.C
- **Speaker:** Martin Luther King Jr
- **Famous phrase:** "I have a dream"
- **Central message:** Equality for all Americans regardless of race

NAME: Rosie W

Capitalization pARTS Student Sample

The next iteration added key information text next to the image—brief facts that contained opportunities to apply multiple capitalization rules. This provided scaffolding while still requiring students to identify which capitalization rules applied to which words.

As with other pARTS protocols, the real power emerged through repetition. Each time students completed the protocol with a new image and information set, they reinforced their understanding of the rules and developed greater automaticity. The consistency of the framework allowed them to focus on application rather than relearning the structure each time.

**Marlena**

If the image makes you laugh, pause, or say, "Ooh"—you've already won. That spark is what pulls kids into the task. Mark's scaffolding sharpens the runway so kids can take off without hesitation.

> **Jon**
>
> Mark's prep has also shrunk: five funny memes or pics, one per day. He's prepped for a week of eight to ten standards per day. Done and done.

> **Mark**
>
> Capitalization pARTS works on paper or digitally, with the only difference being how kids share out. Design for as much flexibility as possible.

## Icon and Template Design

Following the established pARTS naming convention created immediate recognition for students already familiar with 8 pARTS or Sentence pARTS. The visual design maintained the signature pARTS look with "Capitalization" in blue and "ARTS" featuring a prominent "A" in dark gray, to emphasize the ARTS component of pARTS.

Capitalization pARTS Icon

In designing the template, I hoped to maintain a clean, minimalist approach. Each rule was clearly numbered and stated simply, with ample space for student examples. The right side contains space for the visual prompt and supporting information. I chose the darker gray to add a little weight and balance the layout. My hope was that the template would guide students through the process while allowing for personalization.

## Academic Goals

Through successful implementation of Capitalization pARTS, students should:

- Master the six fundamental capitalization rules.
- Develop automaticity in applying capitalization in context.
- Transfer capitalization skills to their independent writing.
- Build critical thinking skills by identifying rule applications in authentic text.
- Connect visual information to written language conventions.

Capitilization pARTS Template

## Teacher Big Ideas

- Focus on application over memorization.
- Build from simple to complex visual prompts.
- Use engaging, relevant images that connect to current content.

One image or source  +  6 Capitalization Rules - 1 sentence each  +  Share out in small group

**PRO TIP:** Add some text to the image that provides material for the different capitalization rules.

Captilization pARTS Recipe Card

## Prepare for the Activity

1. Select a visual prompt that connects with the desired topic and naturally incorporates multiple capitalization opportunities.
2. Create or curate brief information text to accompany each image.
3. Plan for progression from simple to more complex applications.
4. Consider how to incorporate peer feedback, discussion, or AI.

## Instructions

1. Begin with a Smart Start using a familiar image and simple information text. I used students' own birthdays as an initial Smart Start.
2. Review the six capitalization rules briefly.
3. Model identifying words from the information text that exemplify each rule.
4. Have students complete their template, finding examples for each rule.
5. Use Flippity or another random selector for students to share examples.
6. Guide discussion about challenging applications or areas of confusion.
7. Over time, progress to having students create their own information text.

## Key Points to Remember

- Consistency is crucial—initially use the protocol regularly (daily or three times a week for best results).
- Vary image contexts to ensure practice with all rules.
- Connect to authentic writing immediately after practice.

- Look for transfer to independent writing.
- Maintain focus on application rather than definition of rules.

## Variations

- Nacho Paragraph: Provide text with deliberate capitalization errors for students to identify and correct.
- Peer challenge: Students create information text for partners to analyze.
- Cross-curricular connection: Use content-specific images from science, history, or literature.
- Publication prep: Use the protocol as a prepublication checklist for student writing.

The effectiveness of Capitalization pARTS lies in its simplicity and repeatability. What I learned from designing my first EduProtocol was that sometimes the most fundamental skills benefit most from the EduProtocol approach. The structure, repetition, and engagement factors address the exact elements that traditional grammar instruction often lacks.

### Your Turn

What basic skill do your students struggle to apply consistently? How might you adapt the pARTS framework to address this need? Consider how visual prompts might bridge the gap between knowledge and application in your specific context.

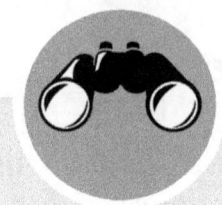

# Chapter 7
## StoryScan EduProtocol

**StoryScan brings together all the essential elements of fiction analysis into one engaging, comprehensive EduProtocol that speaks both academic and student languages.** It transforms what could be a dry analysis of literary elements into an experience that connects traditional learning with youth culture, helping students see how all the pieces of great storytelling work together.

This slide deck includes StoryScan recipe cards, templates, Smart Starts and student samples.

## Design Story

You know that moment when you realize you've been doing something the hard way for years? That's exactly how StoryScan came to be. For almost twenty-five years, I taught the elements of fiction the way most of us probably learned them—one piece at a time, all in isolation. Character analysis this week, setting the next, then on to point of view. Each year I continued to refine my process and lessons and visuals.

The biggest jump I made was in incorporating the BookaKucha EduProtocol as a way for students to share their understanding of each element of fiction. BookaKucha is an EduProtocol where students create a five-to-ten-second share-out about a book, forcing them to distill their thinking into concise, compelling messages while building summarization and public speaking skills. BookaKucha upped both the engagement and output significantly. My students began to more effectively grasp each concept. I began wondering if kids could put elements together so that they could see the bigger picture of how all these pieces worked together. After all, the function of each of these elements is to create a tapestry of storytelling.

One morning, I was standing in front of the class, looking out at glazed eyes as I explained internal conflict for the umpteenth time, and I wondered . . . How might I better engage my students with this isolated element? How might I bring together all these overlapping fiction standards? I reflected on the other EPs, such as 8 pARTS and Comma pARTS, and how those EPs playfully brought all parts together. Could that work for a novel? The 8 pARTS EP covers all the parts of speech in one protocol. What if we tackled *all* the elements of fiction at once, in a way that helped students better see the novel as a whole? Could we perhaps map them in a holistic, engaging, and playful way?

## Design Iterations

The first version of StoryScan was what you'd expect from a veteran teacher: structured, thorough, and to be honest, pretty dry. It covered the bases—author, genre, characters, internal and external conflict, point of view, theme, setting. Technically sound, but something was definitely missing. It just felt like a cleanly designed worksheet. This definitely wasn't yet an EduProtocol.

One leap started from a family text thread about vacation plans, which included inside jokes and movies we had watched. There we were, rapid-fire texting emojis, debating movie reviews, and referencing Rotten Tomatoes scores. That's when I thought that for StoryScan to take the next step, it needed to better speak the language of my students.

I began by adding the three-word summary from 8 pARTS. This added some humor, using caveman-speak to produce a simple summary. After a few more reps, I was looking to add more sizzle and find a better way for students to share out. This was when I added the emoji plot summary alongside the three-word summary.

I also wanted to create space for student opinion and voice while ensuring I was getting them to back up their opinions with some evidence. This was where the stars and tomatoes rating system came in, mimicking the review formats my students were already familiar with. After many reps and iterations, the protocol was coming alive.

**Jon**

Here's a fun fact. There are seven semantic demands to reading: visualizing, monitoring, inferencing (including predicting), identifying important information, generating and answering questions, synthesizing, and summarizing—and almost no teachers teach these all at once. I'm sure the logic of this is divide and conquer, but unless we have kids do all of these at the same time, their reading will progress so slowly that it's painful to watch.

## StoryScan Template

| STORYSCAN | NAME | BOOK | AUTHOR | GENRE |
|---|---|---|---|---|
| | | | | |

| EMOJI PLOT SUMMARY | THREE-WORD PLOT SUMMARY |
|---|---|
| | |

| CHARACTERS | | | SETTING | |
|---|---|---|---|---|
| ROUND | FLAT | | TOWN or AREA | |
| | | IMAGE | PART OF WORLD | |
| | | | KIND OF WORLD | |
| | | | REVIEW | |
| INTERNAL CONFLICT | POV | EXPLANATION | |
| | | | |
| EXTERNAL CONFLICT | THEME | | |
| | | | |

*StoryScan Template*

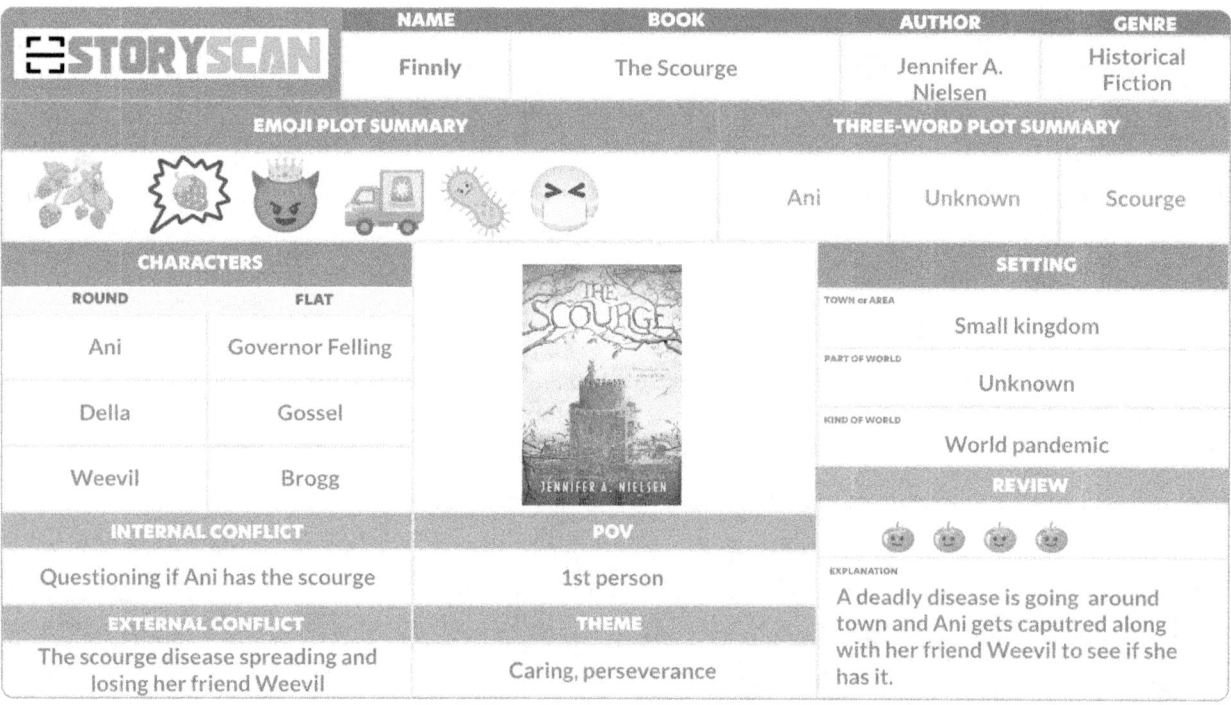

*StoryScan Student Sample*

To add a feedback loop, I used a format similar to the BookaKucha share-out, where each student had twenty seconds to tell us about their book. In this scenario I had them begin with a plot summary using the emojis. The share-out became a combination of book previews, reviews, and an opportunity to assess comprehension and summarizing.

## Icon and Template Design

This evolving EduProtocol needed a name. I wanted to find the sizzle but also stay intentional.

At first, I considered the idea of students being fiction detectives as they read their novels. This was the genesis of the protocol's first name, Fiction Forensics. I worried, though, that this might imply genre-specific fiction, so I continued playing with the name.

Name Iteration #1

> **Marlena**
> The emojis add a visual representation for retelling and comprehension of the story or event, an important addition for many students that allows think time to see the story their own way.

> **Jon**
> I love how Mark is thinking like a scientist or advertising executive in this part of the process. In education, we don't let things breathe enough. We can always take a while to let things evolve so that they are fully baked.

What I eventually realized was that this protocol really fit in the pARTS family. I loved the emphasis on the ARTS component of these EduProtocols, especially after bringing in the emoji retell. However, I didn't want to overuse the pARTS name and have students blur them together.

Name Iteration #2

Later, after I'd had some medical tests and was looking at my results and trying to read them holistically, the protocol came to mind, and the idea of "scanning" hit me. Thus the name StoryScan came to be.

**STORYSCAN**

Final Name and Icon Design

In designing the icon, I tried to imply that this protocol would be like a scan to map fiction, resulting in comprehensive results and a holistic view of the novel.

## Academic Goals

Through successful implementation of StoryScan, students should:

- See how pieces of a story fit together as an integrated whole.
- Develop confidence in analyzing fiction from multiple angles.
- Master expressing complex ideas both traditionally and through modern communication.
- Build critical thinking skills by examining how different story elements interact.
- Connect classroom learning with real-world media literacy.

## Teacher Big Ideas

- Connect traditional literary analysis with youth culture.
- Balance academic requirements with choice.
- Help students see connections between individual elements and the bigger literary picture.
- Encourage both analysis and creativity.
- Value both formal expression and student-centered communication.

# Chapter 7 | StoryScan EduProtocol | 55

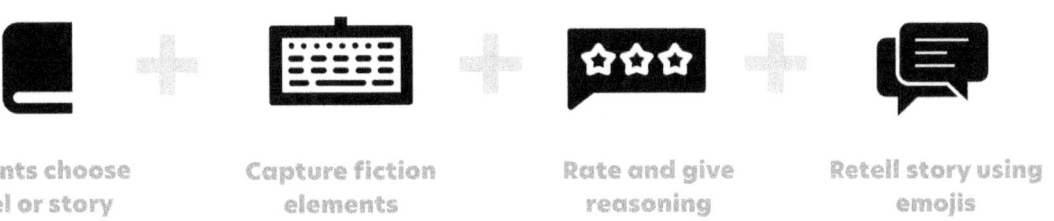

StoryScan Recipe Card

## Prepare for the Activity

1. Select your text carefully for a Smart Start. I recommend using a simple picture book or a whole read aloud that you have finished. Choose something with clear literary elements and enough complexity to generate discussion.
2. Duplicate the template or create your own!
3. Complete the Smart Start template together.
4. Students then select their own novel to read.
5. Students complete a StoryScan analysis on a shared slide deck.
6. Each student gets twenty seconds to share the plot of their book using emojis.

## Instructions

1. Spend time introducing the elements of fiction.

2. Use the BookaKucha EduProtocol, from *The EduProtocol Field Guide: Book 1* by Marlena Hebern and Jon Corippo, to reflect on each element and practice the twenty-second presentation.
3. Challenge students to create their three-word plot summary, pushing them to distill the essence of the story.
4. Introduce the emoji plot summary component, demonstrating how to select emojis that capture key plot points and emotional moments.
5. Have students assign and justify their star rating or tomato score using specific textual evidence.

## Key Points to Remember

Remember that StoryScan works best when you:

- Value both traditional and modern forms of expression.
- Keep the focus on connections between elements.
- Encourage evidence-based reasoning, even with emojis.
- Allow time for discussion and sharing.
- Maintain high expectations while embracing youth culture.

## Variations

- Comparative Analysis: Complete StoryScan for two different works, then compare and contrast.
- Book Talk Springboard: Use a completed StoryScan as the foundation for engaging book talks.
- Creative Writing Launch: Have students use the StoryScan elements as a planning guide for their own stories.
- Group Analysis Gallery: Create poster-sized analyses to display and discuss.
- Progressive Analysis: Build the analysis over time as students read, adding elements as they appear in the text.

On the first share-out using the StoryScan EP, I watched a student explain *The Giver* by Lois Lowry in twenty seconds using nothing but emojis, and you know what? It was one of the most insightful analyses I've seen. StoryScan isn't just another way to teach literature—it's a bridge between the timeless elements of storytelling and the way our students naturally communicate today.

## Your Turn

The evolution of StoryScan demonstrates how traditional teaching approaches can be reimagined as integrated frameworks. What other content or concepts do you typically teach in isolation that might benefit from integration? Consider how you might apply the design principles behind StoryScan to create your own EduProtocol that combines multiple elements into a cohesive framework. What youth culture elements might you incorporate as feedback loops?

# Chapter 8
# Echo Chamber EduProtocol

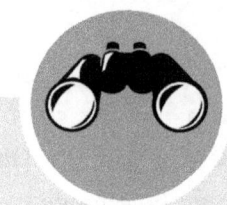

**E**cho Chamber transforms the way students explore different perspectives by having them create and analyze fictional dialogues. Through the creative process of crafting conversations between historical figures, literary characters, or conceptual viewpoints, students develop deeper understanding while engaging in an authentic form of written expression that mirrors their daily communication styles.

This slide deck includes Echo Chamber recipe cards, templates, Smart Starts and student samples.

## Design Story

The process of creating Echo Chamber began as I was trying to get kids more engaged with the characters in their novels. Traditional character analysis of physical traits and emotional characteristics had been effective in some ways, but it often felt a bit static and surface level. Many of the characters were so well written and felt so real, but student descriptions of the characters remained so basic. For example, instead of analyzing how characters drive the plot, students would write surface observations like "The main character is a teenage girl who was adopted." I wanted to find a deeper way for students to think about them.

Students spend a lot of time messaging their friends. They don't mind carefully choosing words and emojis to convey meaning. They even tend to overread into the nuances of text messages and infer tone and meaning. I began to wonder, "What if I could

**Jon**

It's exciting to see Mark went through the same thought process I did with dialogue. Nearly all teachers teach what I'd call quotation marks and the basics, but I cannot recall being taught *dialogue*. That interaction aspect. For me, adding dialogue to Sentence pARTS was eye-opening. After a few reps, kids were even doing split quotes—because it made sense.

tap into that aspect of youth culture and have students generate dialogue to deepen their understanding of literature?"

That's when the first version, called Book Bubbles, was born. Book Bubbles was a simple way for students to imagine and create conversations between characters from their reading. Students connected with the format because it reflected their daily communication. Through generating fictional conversations based on their reading and understanding of characters, they were moving beyond *describing* characters and toward *analyzing* characters by trying to imagine how their character might think and communicate, bringing them to life through dialogue that felt authentic and engaging.

## Design Iterations

The first versions of this protocol were purely focused on literary analysis, asking students to create conversations between characters from their novels. I waffled on names. TextTalk? Dialogue Portal? Ultimately, I landed on Book Bubbles. I liked it. It was simple, alliterative, catchy, and descriptive.

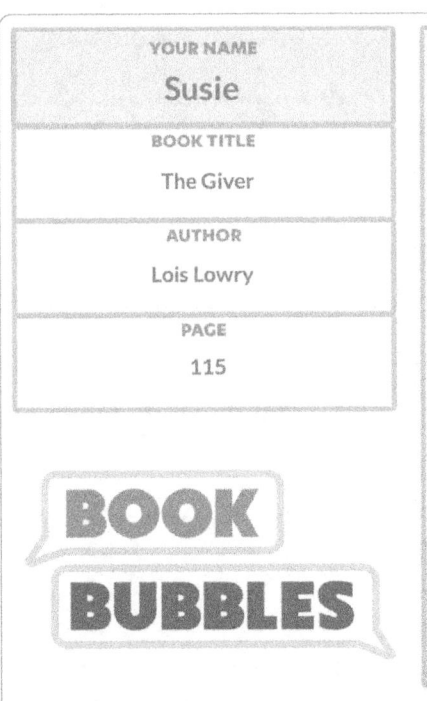 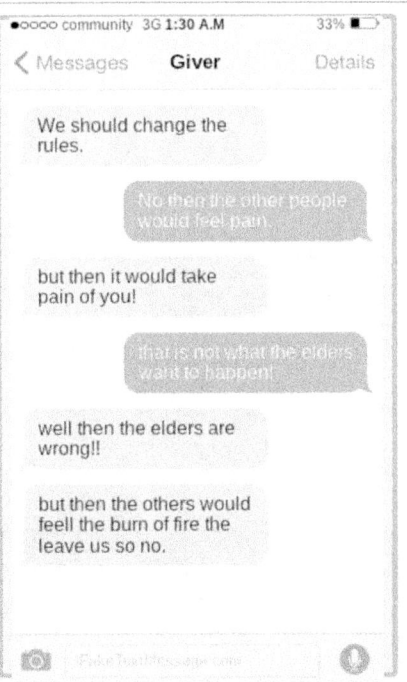

Student sample in a literary study.

However, later in that same school year, during a lesson on major figures of the American Revolution, we were talking as a class about the significance of media and print during this time period—and the power (but slow pace) of word-of-mouth communication. Randomly, we were discussing how things would have been different had the internet been available and what might it have sounded like if these figures had had cell phones. This got me thinking back to Book Bubbles. If students could bring fictional characters to life through dialogue, why not historical figures? I tried having students create a conversation between a Founding Father and King George III, and the results were quite insightful. We repeated the process again with George Washington and his soldiers following the encampment at Valley Forge. Students weren't just memorizing historical facts—they were engaging with different perspectives and motivations.

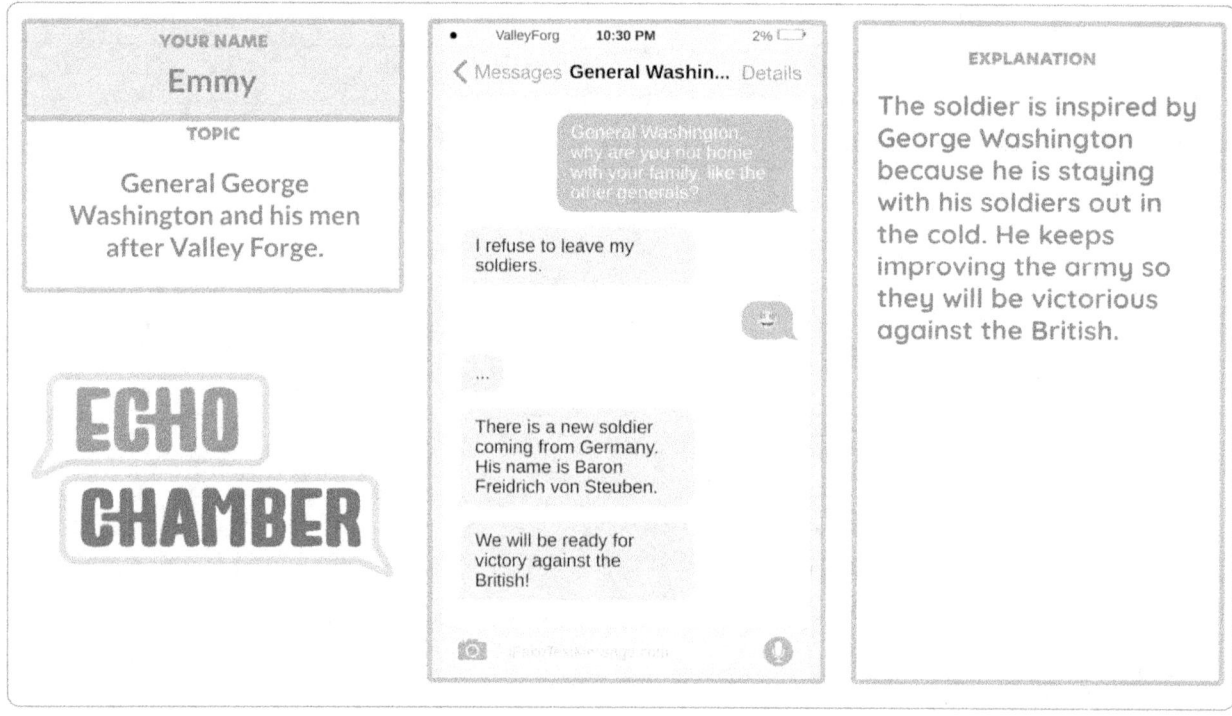

Student sample in historical study.

This cross-curricular moment led to the protocol's evolution into Echo Chamber. The name change reflected how the protocol had become a space to hear voices from different times, places, and perspectives—like distant echoes coming together in conversation.

The dialogue became the creative expression of multiple perspectives, and the explanation was the opportunity for students to support their dialogue choices with evidence from a text or facts they had learned. It wasn't a silly conversation but a platform to show deeper understanding.

We then began using a website called ifaketextmessage.com to create realistic-looking dialogue boxes, though the protocol worked just as well using callout boxes when our district filter suddenly blocked the site.

**Marlena**
Simple yet powerful. A perfect EduProtocol!

**Mark**
Our district blocking the fake text website was peak educational irony—we ban the communication tools students live in, then scratch our heads about engagement problems.

## Icon and Template Design

The evolution from Book Bubbles to Echo Chamber reflected the protocol's expansion beyond just literary analysis. The name *Echo Chamber* captures the essence of what happens when we create these dialogues—when we create space where we can hear snippets of conversation from different perspectives, times, and places, like faint echoes reaching across distance or time. The logo design is intentionally simple, using dialogue bubbles to remind students of the conversational nature of the protocol.

Name Iteration #1

Final Name and Icon Design

The template was designed to fit a phone-sized message thread and add some space for students to explain their thinking. It's radically simple and minimalist, but student thinking is elevated.

Echo Chamber Template

## Academic Goals

Through successful implementation of Echo Chamber, students should:

- Demonstrate deep understanding of multiple perspectives.
- Create authentic dialogue that reflects character or historical figure viewpoints.
- Support dialogue choices with evidence and reasoning.
- Analyze relationships and conflicts between different viewpoints.
- Practice clear written expression in both dialogue and explanation.

## Teacher Big Ideas

- Embrace the natural way students communicate through messaging.
- Balance creative expression with academic rigor.
- Focus on the reasoning behind dialogue choices.
- Use familiar formats to explore complex ideas.
- Value both the creation and analysis of dialogue.

 +  +  +

Choose 2 characters or figures | Generate fictional dialogue | Support conversation with reasoning | Share dialogue in small groups

**KEY IDEA:** The beauty of the student thinking often shows up in the "why" rather than in the actual dialogue. Emphasize the explanation.

Echo Chamber Recipe Card

## Prepare for the Activity

1. Choose your method: digital (using ifaketextmessage.com or callouts on Google Slides) or analog (paper templates).
2. Select appropriate paired perspectives (characters, historical figures, concepts).
3. Prepare examples showing both strong dialogue and thoughtful analysis.
4. Create clear expectations for both dialogue creation and explanation.
5. Plan your sharing method (gallery walk, readers theater, small groups).

## Instructions

1. Introduce the perspectives students will be working with.
2. Model the creation of a dialogue, explaining your choices.
3. Have students draft their conversations, focusing on authentic voice.
4. Guide students in analyzing their dialogue choices.
5. Facilitate sharing through your chosen method.
6. Lead reflection on the perspectives explored.

## Key Points to Remember

- Value creativity in dialogue creation.
- Require evidence-based explanations of choices.
- Allow appropriate voice and language for characters.
- Focus on the reasoning behind dialogue choices.
- Keep the fun in the process while maintaining academic rigor.

## Variations

- Historical Conversations: Create dialogues between historical figures.
- Literary Analysis: Explore character relationships through messaging.
- Scientific Debate: Create dialogues between scientists with different theories.
- Mathematical Reasoning: Show problem-solving through conversation.
- Cross-Cultural Communication: Explore different cultural perspectives.
- Contemporary Issues: Examine multiple viewpoints on current events.

The power of Echo Chamber lies in its ability to make distant voices feel immediate and relevant. If students can craft a conversation between Abraham Lincoln and Frederick Douglass, or between Scout Finch and Boo Radley, they are truly engaging with these perspectives in a way that traditional analysis rarely achieves. They're not just studying history or literature anymore—they're participating in conversations across time and space.

### Your Turn

Echo Chamber transformed traditional character analysis by tapping into youth culture. What other content areas might benefit from this approach? How might you design a protocol that leverages familiar youth culture elements to connect to the content?

# Chapter 9
## ReRoute EduProtocol

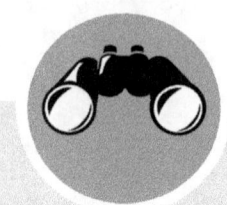

This slide deck includes ReRoute recipe cards, templates, Smart Starts and student samples.

**E**very classroom has its unique dynamics, but some universal truths emerge when we work with young people who are still developing social skills and impulse control. ReRoute is an SEL EduProtocol that emerged from the challenge of helping students understand how their choices affect others. Rather than focusing on "correcting misbehavior," this protocol helps students analyze choices through the lens of basic needs and guides them toward more effective ways to meet those needs.

## Design Story

The genesis of ReRoute came from a particularly impulsive group of boys in my classroom. These students were genuinely good-natured kids who brought incredible energy and humor to our classroom community. Many of them were avid YouTube watchers (to say it in the most positive way I can) and seemed to have an insatiable drive to meet their own need for fun and belonging. This was a very neurodiverse group, which sometimes increased the complexity of reading social cues or understanding how some of their impulsive choices were impacting others. After some challenges at specialists, some growing parent concerns, and seeing my classroom community starting to suffer, I wondered if there might be a way to tap into the success I was experiencing with current EduProtocols, but in the space of social-emotional growth.

I knew that traditional approaches might get me a reduction in negative behavior, but they weren't going to produce the long-

**Jon**
Just having kids "not get in trouble" or suppress their impulses isn't working in the long term. When we want kids to change, we need to entice them with an engaging *alternative* way of working at school.

term intrinsic change I was hoping for. Traditional behavior management focuses on external rewards or punishments and misses a crucial element: understanding the fundamental needs driving behavior choices. Drawing from my background in choice theory, I knew that all behavior is purposeful and is an attempt to meet one or more of the five basic needs: survival, love and belonging, power, freedom, or fun. The question became this: How might I help students recognize these needs and find better ways to meet them?

## BASIC NEEDS

BELONGING · FUN · POWER / SUCCESS · FREEDOM · SURVIVAL

Based on Control Theory by William Glasser

## Design Iterations

The first version of ReRoute was straightforward but incomplete. We began by examining fictional situations (many times crafted to mirror real classroom scenarios without singling anyone out), and students would identify which of the basic needs they thought were driving the behavior and what unintended consequences resulted. Then, they would brainstorm healthier alternatives for meeting those same needs.

**Mark**

Traditional behavior management asks, "How do we stop this behavior?" ReRoute asks, "How do we empower students to meet their needs in a more positive way?" These are *different* outcomes.

68 | Designing EduProtocols

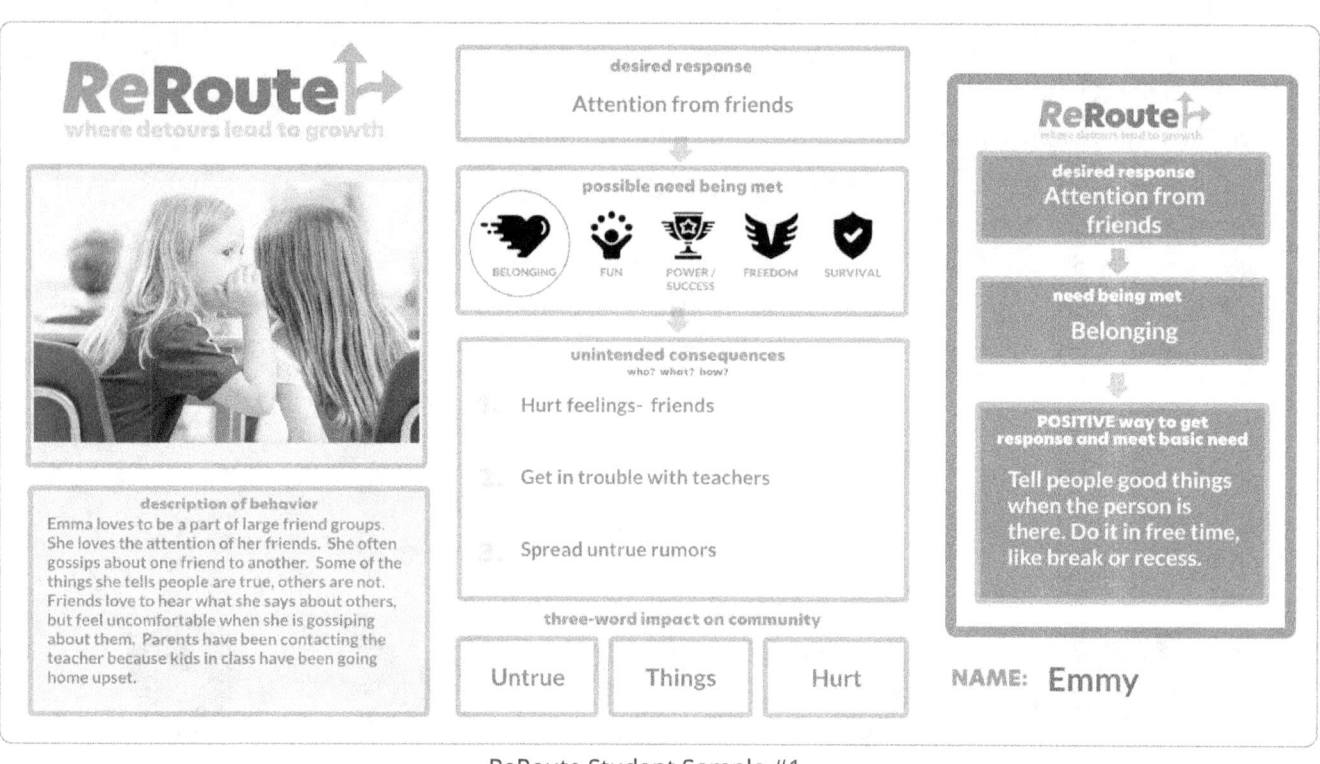

ReRoute Student Sample #1

This process showed promise with the repetitions, but something was missing. Students struggled with bridging the gap between the intention behind a behavior and its impact. That's when I added the *desired responses* section, aiming to help students articulate what they thought the person was hoping would happen. This simple addition created somewhat of an aha moment—students began recognizing that even good intentions could still lead to problematic outcomes.

The protocol took another leap forward when I introduced the *three-word impact on community* element. Using the three-word caveman-speak of the 8 pARTS EduProtocol added an element of creativity and levity to what could often be more serious discussions. Students began coming up with creative and insightful three-word summaries like "fun makes chaos" or "joke hurts feelings," capturing complex situations in accessible ways.

The final piece came with the visual representation of the five basic needs through simple icons. Having students circle or star the

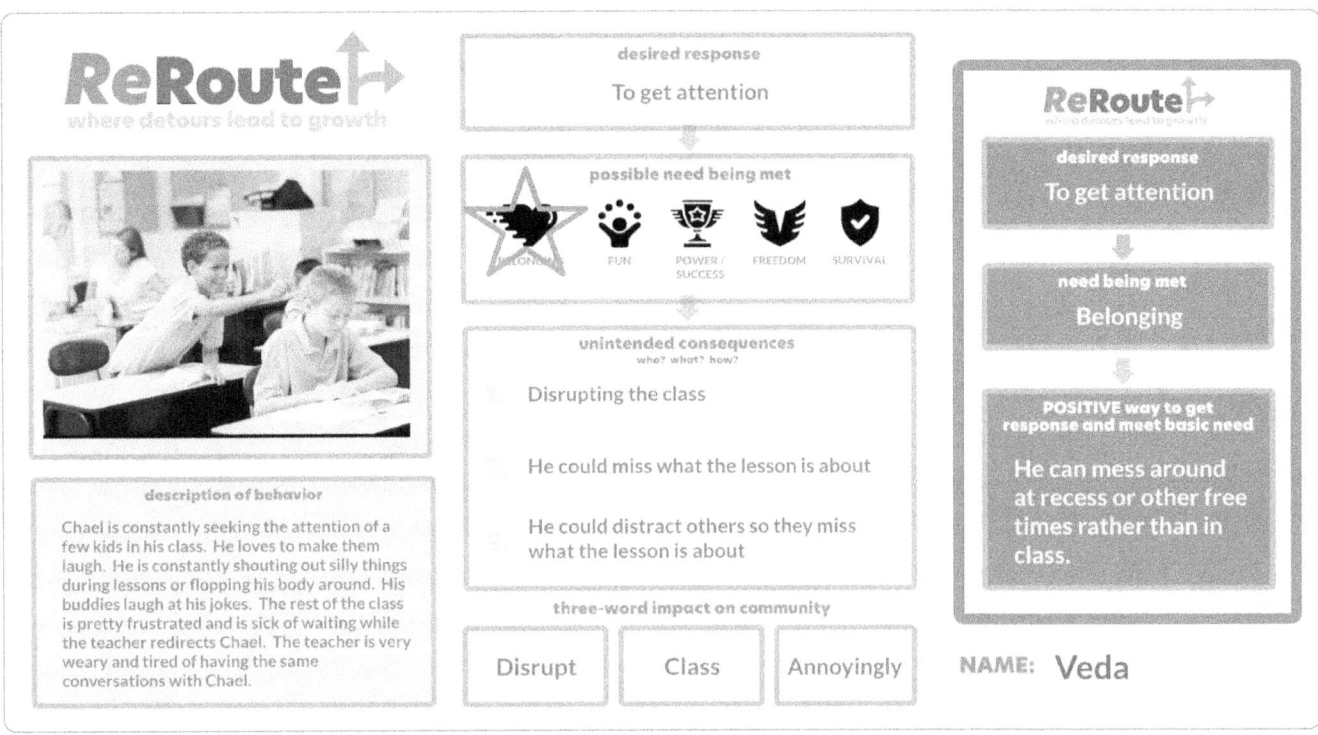

ReRoute Student Sample #2

needs they identified made the analysis more concrete and helped reinforce their understanding of these fundamental concepts.

## Icon and Template Design

I had a hard time naming this one. I wanted the name to be both descriptive and catchy but not sound overly academic or punitive. After all, the goal was to help lead students to make more informed and empathic choices, not shame them for their mistakes. I dabbled with names like Choice Chain and Impact Investigator to stay alliterative, but those felt corny. I wanted to focus most on the unintended impact of impulsive choices. I tried Ripple Reader but felt that it was too abstract. Behavior Bridge was a possibility, but the word *behavior* had pretty strong negative connotations for my students.

In addition, so many of my students seemed to be getting stuck in the binary of whether they were "in trouble" or "not in trouble," when what I was hoping for was a more expansive thought process. The name ReRoute actually came to my mind because of a scene in *Terminator 2* where Arnold Schwarzenegger's character is seemingly defeated but then reroutes power in a different, more effective direction. This is what I wanted for my students. Not to squelch or punish them, but to help them see how behavior choices impact others so they could reroute those choices and have their basic needs met in a more positive way.

Final ReRoute Icon Design. The tagline is especially meanigful to me because it emphaisized the heart behind the EduProtocol.

The template didn't flow well at first. Students weren't seeing the interconnected nature or flow. I added some color variations and arrows to try and guide their thinking.

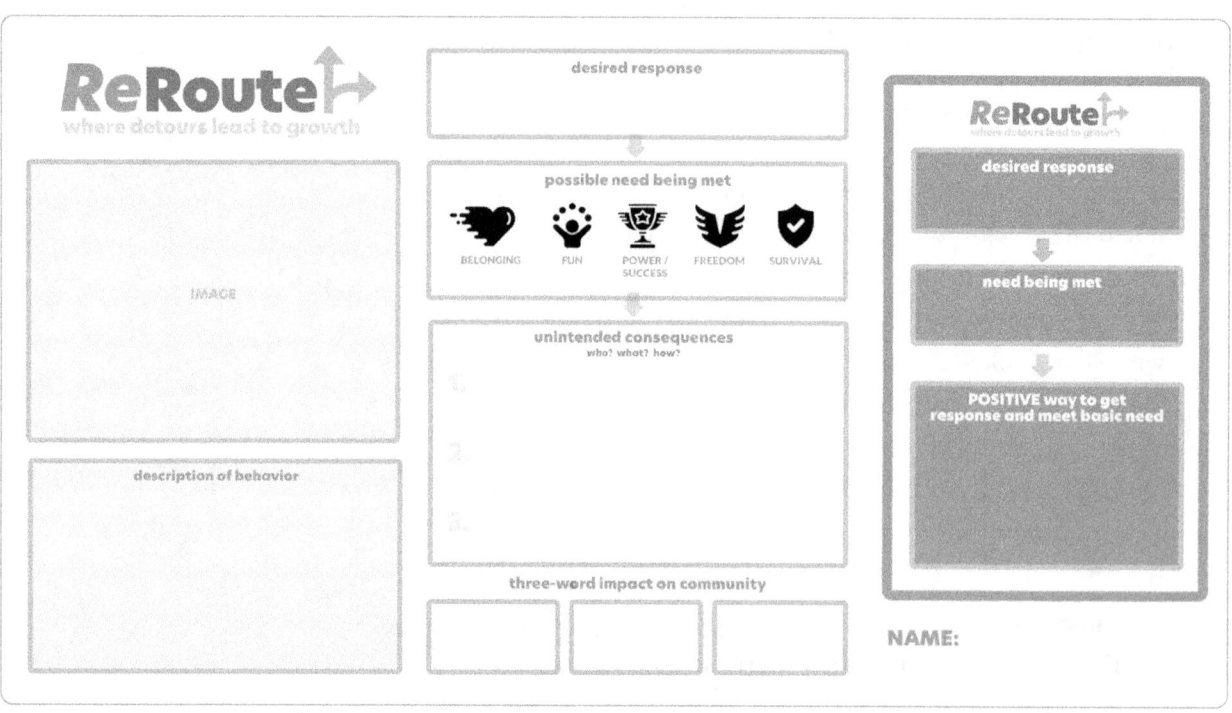

ReRoute Template

# ReRoute in Action: A Classroom Example

One ongoing challenge in my classroom was the tendency for some students to impulsively shout out jokes or comments aimed at getting laughs from their peers. While their intention was to create fun and connection, the impact was often quite different.

Here's how we applied the ReRoute EduProtocol to this situation.

## 1. Scenario Presented to Class

I described a scenario that resembled real situations we'd experienced in our classroom: "During a class discussion, a student suddenly shouts, 'That answer was so long, like your forehead!' Several students laugh."

## 2. Desired Responses Identified by Students

- "They wanted people to think they're funny."
- "They wanted to get attention from the class."
- "They were trying to connect with other students."

## 3. Basic Needs Circled

- Fun (most common)
- Power (a few students identified this)
- Belonging (many identified this)

## 4. Unintended Consequences

- The targeted student felt embarrassed.
- Class discussion was interrupted.
- The teacher had to stop teaching to address the situation.
- Some students felt worried they might be next.

### 5. Three-Word Impact

- "Jokes hurt feelings"
- "Fun creates fear"
- "Laughs damage community"

### 6. Alternative Solutions

- Ensure jokes are reserved for close friends who feel safe.
- Save jokes for recess or social time.
- Write down funny thoughts to share at appropriate times.
- Share a joke with friends during class transitions.
- Focus humor on situations, not on people.

## Academic Goals

Through successful implementation of ReRoute, students should:

- Understand the five basic needs and how they drive behavior.
- Develop empathy by considering others' perspectives.
- Analyze the relationship between intentions and impact.
- Create alternative solutions that meet needs appropriately.
- Build social awareness and community consciousness.

## Connections to SEL Standards

ReRoute naturally aligns with the CASEL (Collaborative for Academic, Social, and Emotional Learning) framework's core competencies:

1. Self-awareness: Students identify their own needs and recognize how their behavior attempts to meet those needs.
2. Self-management: Students develop strategies to redirect impulses toward positive outcomes for all.
3. Social awareness: The protocol explicitly builds empathy by analyzing how behavior impacts others.

4. Relationship skills: Students practice communicating needs appropriately and resolving interpersonal conflicts.
5. Responsible decision-making: The entire ReRoute process guides students to make constructive choices about personal behavior.

These connections make ReRoute valuable not just as a behavior management approach but as a valuable tool to meet educational standards for social-emotional learning.

**Marlena**

I love this! The ReRoute EduProtocol takes a purposeful step toward creating classroom community by building capacity for empathy.

## Teacher Big Ideas

- Focus on understanding rather than judgment.
- Keep scenarios fictional but relevant.
- Use humor and creativity to maintain engagement.
- Build a safe space for honest discussion.
- Emphasize that all needs are valid—it's the method of meeting them that might need adjustment.

 +   +   +

Present students with a problem or scenario   Identify desired response and basic needs   Brainstorm unintended consequences   Generate positive ways to meet basic needs

**KEY IDEA:** This EduProtocol is not about shaming or blaming. Instead, focus on empowering students to make choices that make a positive impact.

ReRoute Recipe Card

## Prepare for the Activity

1. Create or collect relevant scenarios that reflect common classroom situations.
2. Prepare visual representations of the five basic needs.
3. Use or modify the template with spaces for the following:
    a. Scenario description
    b. Desired responses
    c. Identified needs (with icons)
    d. Unintended consequences
    e. Three-word community impact
    f. Alternative solutions

## Instructions

1. Present a scenario to the class.
2. Guide students in identifying desired responses.
3. Have students circle relevant basic needs icons.
4. Analyze unintended consequences.
5. Create three-word impact statements.
6. Brainstorm alternative ways to meet the identified needs.
7. Share and discuss potential "reroutes."

## Key Points to Remember

- Keep the tone constructive and solution-focused.
- Avoid singling out specific students.
- Celebrate creative alternatives.
- Maintain a balance between serious analysis and playful expression.
- Reinforce that "rerouting" is about finding better paths, not avoiding needs.

## Differentiation for Various Grade Levels

### Early Elementary (K–2)

- Use simple scenarios with clear cause-effect relationships.
- Incorporate puppets or stuffed animals to act out scenarios.
- Use visual cues throughout the process.
- Focus primarily on identifying feelings of others to build the empathy muscle.

### Upper Elementary (3–5)

- Use scenarios relevant to playground and friendship dynamics.
- Emphasize concrete alternatives that can be immediately applied.
- Have students create their own scenarios based on observed (not personal) situations.

### Middle School

- Add nuance to the needs discussion (e.g., different types of belonging).
- Include scenarios about social media and online behavior.
- Incorporate written reflection components.
- Add deeper discussion of how we infer others' intentions.

### High School

- Connect to broader concepts like implicit bias and systemic thinking.
- Include scenarios about complex social dynamics and future workplace situations.
- Add student-led facilitation after initial modeling.
- Connect to literature, history, and current events.

- Incorporate research on psychological concepts and conflict resolution.

## Measuring Success

How do you know if ReRoute is making a difference? Consider tracking these metrics:

1. Behavioral incidents: Document specific types of behaviors before implementing ReRoute and at regular intervals afterward. Look for decreases in impulsive behaviors and increases in positive alternatives.
2. Student language: Listen for students using ReRoute terminology outside the protocol. When you hear students discussing "needs" or "impacts" in natural conversation, it signals internalization.
3. Reflection sophistication: Collect samples of student work from early ReRoute sessions and compare with later implementations. Look for increased complexity in students' thinking about intentions, impacts, and alternatives. Remember . . . repetition!
4. Self-referrals: Notice when students begin to voluntarily apply the ReRoute process to their own behavior. This self-regulation indicates deep integration of the concepts.
5. Classroom climate surveys: Implement brief, anonymous surveys asking students how safe they feel expressing themselves in class. Administer them before implementing ReRoute and periodically thereafter.
6. Peer mediation quality: If you use peer mediation in your classroom, track how students incorporate ReRoute concepts into helping their classmates resolve conflicts.

Remember that meaningful change takes time. The goal isn't immediate perfection but steady progress toward increased awareness and more intentional choices.

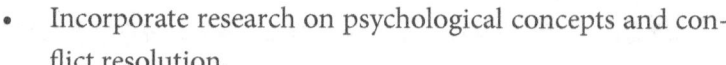

**Marlena**

Any one of these metrics will give you a read on student progress. Want to measure long-term impact? Track one or more of these metrics over a semester—or even the whole year!

## Variations

- Student-Generated Scenarios: Let students anonymously submit situations for analysis.
- Historical ReRoute: Apply the protocol to historical conflicts.
- Literary Analysis: Examine character choices through the ReRoute lens.
- Role-Play ReRoute: Act out alternative solutions.
- Digital ReRoute: Create video examples of scenarios and solutions.

The power of ReRoute lies in its ability to transform what could be punitive behavioral management into a thoughtful exploration of human needs and social impact. When I see students begin to pause before reacting, consider the potential impact of their choices, and find creative ways to meet their needs while respecting others, that moves beyond temporary compliance toward genuine social growth.

### Your Turn

ReRoute demonstrates how EduProtocol design can address social-emotional needs alongside academic goals. What other SEL challenges might benefit from a structured, repeatable protocol approach? Consider how you might design a framework that helps students develop specific social-emotional skills while incorporating elements that make it engaging and relevant to youth culture. What feedback loops would make your EduProtocol most effective?

# Chapter 10
## Word Hunters EduProtocol

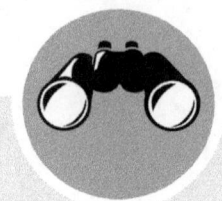

**Word Hunters turns the traditionally dry study of morphology into an EduProtocol that builds students' word analysis skills through discovery, creativity, and play.** By combining systematic word study with elements of gaming and visual thinking, this protocol helps students develop a deeper understanding of how words work while maintaining high levels of engagement.

This slide deck includes Word Hunters recipe cards, templates, Smart Starts and student samples.

Word Hunters naturally addresses multiple language arts standards across grade levels. This protocol directly supports standards related to determining meaning of unknown words, understanding word relationships, and analyzing the role of prefixes, suffixes, and root words in determining word meanings. Beyond vocabulary acquisition, it builds analytical thinking, pattern recognition, and metacognitive awareness of language structure—essential literacy skills that span across curriculum areas.

I've found Word Hunters to be particularly effective with students in the intermediate grades, where vocabulary demands increase dramatically and morphological awareness becomes ever more critical for academic success. The protocol can be modified for different developmental levels—emphasizing common prefixes and suffixes for younger students and incorporating Greek and Latin roots and more complex word relationships for middle schoolers. High school teachers can further adapt it by focusing on domain-specific vocabulary in subjects like science, social studies, and literature.

## Design Story

Sometimes the best teaching ideas emerge from moments of frustration. I was sitting in another professional development session, this time about the upcoming adoption of a new district language arts curriculum. A representative from the curriculum company was brought in to teach us all about student engagement and morphology instruction. The irony was palpable—here we were, a room full of educators being lectured for 120 minutes about engagement while experiencing perhaps the least engaging presentation possible. As I watched colleagues struggle to stay focused during a two-hour talk about the importance of active learning, I couldn't help but think of my students and how they must feel during traditional instruction like this.

I have become more and more aware that morphological awareness—the ability to recognize and manipulate meaningful parts of words—is strongly correlated with reading comprehension, vocabulary development, and overall literacy achievement. I also know that instruction in word parts, like best practices in other areas, needs to be active, inquiry based, and connected to meaningful contexts rather than isolated drills. Word Hunters puts this research into practice by transforming morphology instruction from passive reception of information into active exploration and discovery.

**Jon**

Kids actually *like* practicing. They memorize dinosaurs, Pokémon, and all kinds of details in Fortnite. When we get creative about the work, set it up like a game show and give immediate feedback, the master EduProtocols teacher can make anything fun to learn.

**Marlena**

The reversed nature of Word Hunters puts students squarely in the driver's seat of vocabulary acquisition. It's about time!

## Design Iterations

The first version of Word Hunters revealed both promise and limitations. After some explicit instruction, my thought was to have students tune into their independent reading and find words that exemplified the use of prefixes, roots, and suffixes that we were learning. They would find a word, break it into its parts, define each part, and then add an image or GIF that exemplified that part.

Students who already had a strong foundation in recognizing prefixes, suffixes, and roots did well right away with the freedom to hunt for words in their own novels. However, about half of my students struggled with this open-ended approach, unable to consistently identify word parts on their own. They simply lacked the experience, and I realized that identifying words was an additional skill beyond breaking down words.

This observation led to the first major iteration: providing a shared word for the whole class to analyze together. In addition, I curated a few links to help students define prefixes, suffixes, and roots that they didn't know. This simplification and scaffolding helped level the playing field.

The next iteration introduced brainstorming of related words that shared prefixes and suffixes, along with visual representations to reinforce meaning. This added one more layer of depth to the learning, as students needed to think visually about what their related words meant. But something was still missing—feedback loops and peer interaction.

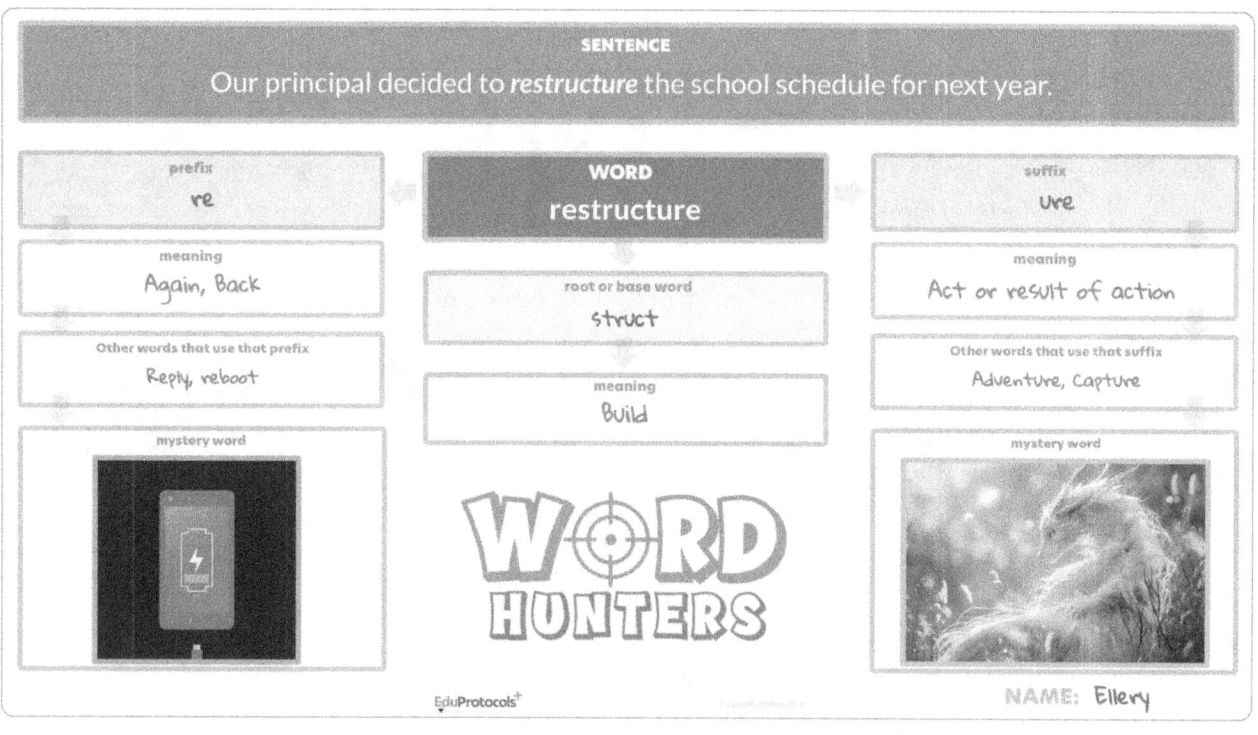

Student sample with the word "unhelpful"

The breakthrough came with the addition of a gamified element. Students defined the word parts and then brainstormed other words that used the same parts. Then, rather than only listing the words, they were asked to pick a word with a shared prefix and one with a shared suffix and keep the words a mystery. They then created visual clues for mystery words using images or GIFs to represent meaning. Then, using Flippity, I randomly selected presenters. Students would come up and share their slide and offer classmates three chances to guess the mystery word that used the same prefix or suffix. The energy in the room transformed—suddenly, morphology became a game of detection and discovery, and students were racking their brains to think of how other words use prefixes and suffixes.

**Marlena**

Analyzing one's own data, experimenting, testing the boundaries, and modifying instruction is the active part of teaching. It's why couch critics get our profession so wrong. It's what good teachers do a thousand times a day. And Mark is showing us how to put all of that into an EduProtocol in real time!

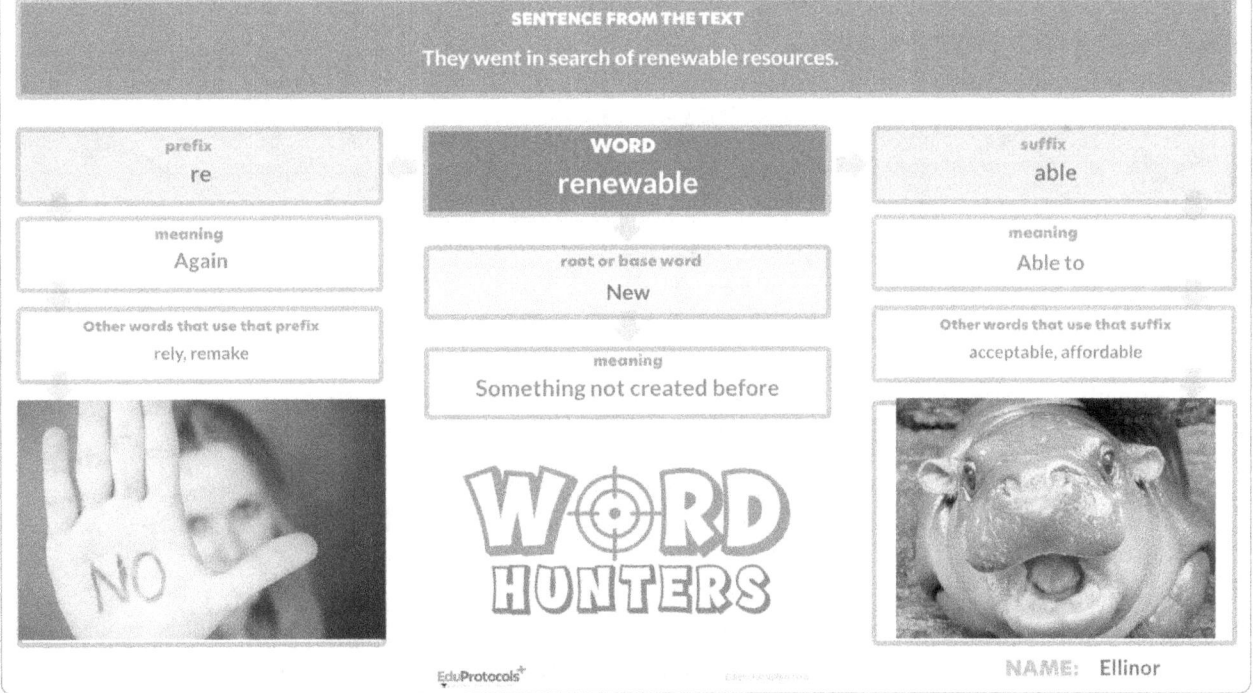

Student sample with the word "renewable"

Through this process, I realized that before students could become independent word hunters, they needed multiple encounters with shared words in an engaging, supportive environment. The

> **Mark**
>
> Silly GIFs as prompts freed students from the pressure of "literary" responses. Sometimes you have to lower the stakes to raise the thinking.

protocol helped build confidence before asking students to venture out on their own word-finding missions.

Word Hunters also naturally integrates authentic assessment into the learning process. While students are engaged in what feels like a word detection game, I'm gathering valuable formative data on their morphological awareness. Students' ability to identify word parts, generate related words, and create visual representations provides immediate insight into their understanding. This allows me to adjust instruction without resorting to traditional assessments that often measure short-term memorization rather than lasting comprehension.

### Icon and Template Design

This name came quickly. I wanted to have students hunt carefully for words. Word Hunters just came out of my mouth. The icon design was inspired by the old Bugs Bunny cartoons. "Be vewy, vewy quiet . . ."

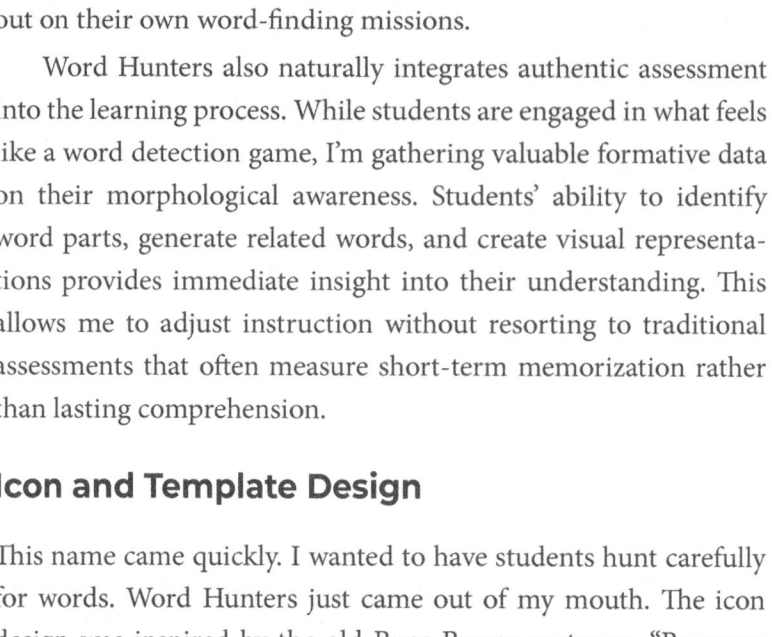

Final Name and Icon Design

This template took a lot of work. There was a lot being asked of the students, and I needed to make the template as uncomplicated as possible while still being intuitive. I'm still not sure it's in its finished state, but it is my best design effort thus far, and students seem to intuitively know what to do.

> **Marlena**
>
> Names make the game! Using fun and creative names is how EduProtocols become memorable for teachers and students.

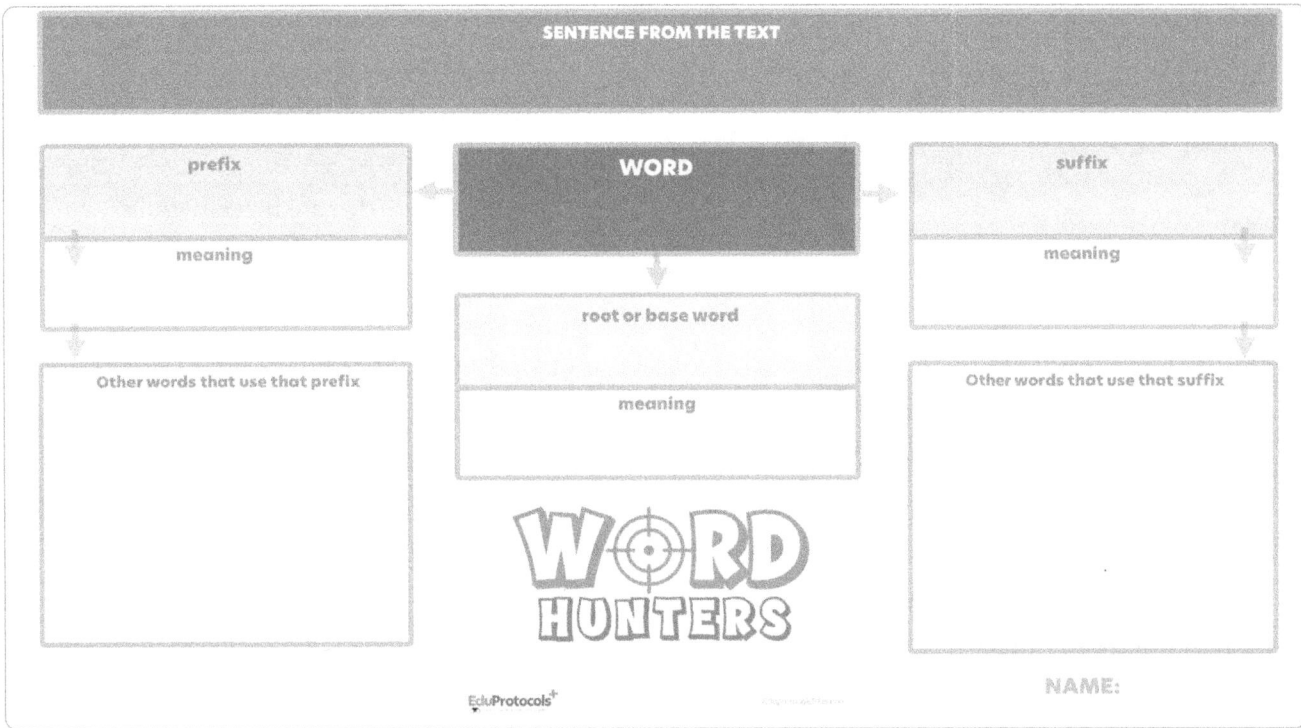

Word Hunters Template

## Academic Goals

Through successful implementation of Word Hunters, students should:

- Develop proficiency in identifying prefixes, suffixes, and roots.
- Build understanding of how word parts contribute to meaning.
- Create meaningful connections between related words.
- Strengthen visual thinking and representation skills.
- Gain confidence in word analysis and morphology.

## Teacher Big Ideas

- Start with shared words before moving to independent hunting.

### Jon

Nothing makes me cringe more than a teacher assigning all 30 words to every student! Fast and Curious: Spot the tricky words. Word Hunters: Dive deeper into select words. Jigsaw: Split the list so students teach each other—cover all words without the overload.

- Build in multiple opportunities for success.
- Use visuals to reinforce meaning.
- Incorporate game elements thoughtfully.
- Balance structure and creativity.
- Ensure every student can participate meaningfully.

 +  +  +  +

Choose a word
(Or have students find words)

Determine meanings of word parts and list examples

Think of mystery word that uses prefix and one for suffix.
Capture those words using image/GIF.

Have other students try and guess the mystery words

**KEY IDEA:** The key is to have students recognize that many words are made up of parts. Knowing the parts can help you determine meaning.

Word Hunters Recipe Card

## Prepare for the Activity

1. Select target words that clearly demonstrate morphological patterns.
2. Gather reliable resources for students to look up the meanings of common prefixes, suffixes, and roots.
3. Set up Flippity or another random selection tool.
4. Use or modify a template for student work.

## Instructions

1. Introduce the shared word and identify its parts together.
2. Guide students in exploring prefix and suffix meanings.
3. Have students find related words using the same word parts.
4. Guide creation of mystery word clues.
5. Facilitate sharing and guessing game.
6. Reflect on word relationships and patterns.

## Key Points to Remember

- Build confidence through structured practice.
- Celebrate creative visual connections.
- Keep the game element lively but focused.
- Support struggling students with word part recognition.
- Maintain engagement through quick-paced sharing.
- Value both accuracy and creativity.

## Variations

- Word Part Tournament: Create bracket-style competitions for best visual clues.
- Word Root Challenge: Create competitions where students compete to find the most words containing specific roots within a time limit.
- Fast and Curious: Connect the word parts into reps in Fast and Curious.

The magic of Word Hunters lies in its ability to transform morphology instruction from "telling" to "exploring." Seeing students eagerly analyzing words, creating clever visual clues, and making connections between word parts makes morphology study more meaningful and memorable.

## Your Turn

Word Hunters evolved through multiple iterations, demonstrating the design process itself. What direct instruction do you currently do that might benefit from reimagining? How might you transform it into a game-based framework that students could use repeatedly across different content? Sketch a preliminary design, knowing that like Word Hunters, your EduProtocol will likely evolve through classroom testing and student feedback.

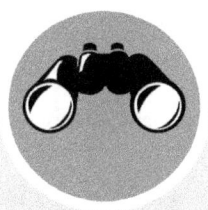

# Chapter 11
# Wordplay Factory EduProtocol

This slide deck includes Wordplay Factory recipe cards, templates, Smart Starts and student samples.

**W**ordplay Factory shifts the traditionally sequential teaching of figurative language into an integrated, engaging experience where students create and master multiple types of figurative language simultaneously. This protocol harnesses the power of generative content learning to help students not only recognize figurative language but confidently create their own.

## Design Story

Like many teachers, I had spent years teaching figurative language types one at a time, carefully scaffolding each concept before moving to the next. We would spend a few days on similes, then metaphors, then personification, having fun with each individual component but creating what felt like artificial boundaries between these naturally interconnected concepts. After experiencing the transformative power of other EduProtocols, I began to question relying on this traditional approach.

The success of protocols like 8 pARTS and Comma pARTS had shown me how students could thrive when given the opportunity to engage with multiple skills simultaneously. I realized that my careful sequencing of figurative language instruction might be limiting student learning rather than supporting it. What if, instead of treating each type of figurative language as a separate

**Jon**

Most teachers will take a month to cover four literary devices because that's what the published curriculum presents to the teacher. But in reality, there are thirty-six common literary devices, and kids need them all. And with an EduProtocol mindset, we can knock all thirty-six out in . . . four weeks.

88 | Designing EduProtocols

challenge to master, we embraced them all at once? Could it work? Or would it result in chaos?

## Design Iterations

The first version of Wordplay Factory was ambitious, admittedly too ambitious. I jumped in with both feet, including eight types of figurative language on the first template: simile, metaphor, personification, hyperbole, allusion, onomatopoeia, connotation, and idiom. I gave students a GIF to analyze and asked them to write an example of figurative language for each. Students were engaged with the content, asking great questions of each other, and successfully produced many of the figurative language examples. However, it quickly became clear that connotation and idiom were going to require more explicit teaching and/or extensive background knowledge than the other types. Kids were confused and frustrated, and I pulled the plug before finishing.

Wordplay Factory Initial Template. This turned out to be too complicated and was a bit of a disaster.

Chapter 11 | Wordplay Factory EduProtocol | 89

I decided to back off a little with the redesign. The next iteration worked more smoothly, focusing only on the six more accessible types. The Smart Starts engaged students by using deliberately silly images and GIFs. The playful nature of these prompts freed students to be more creative with their figurative language.

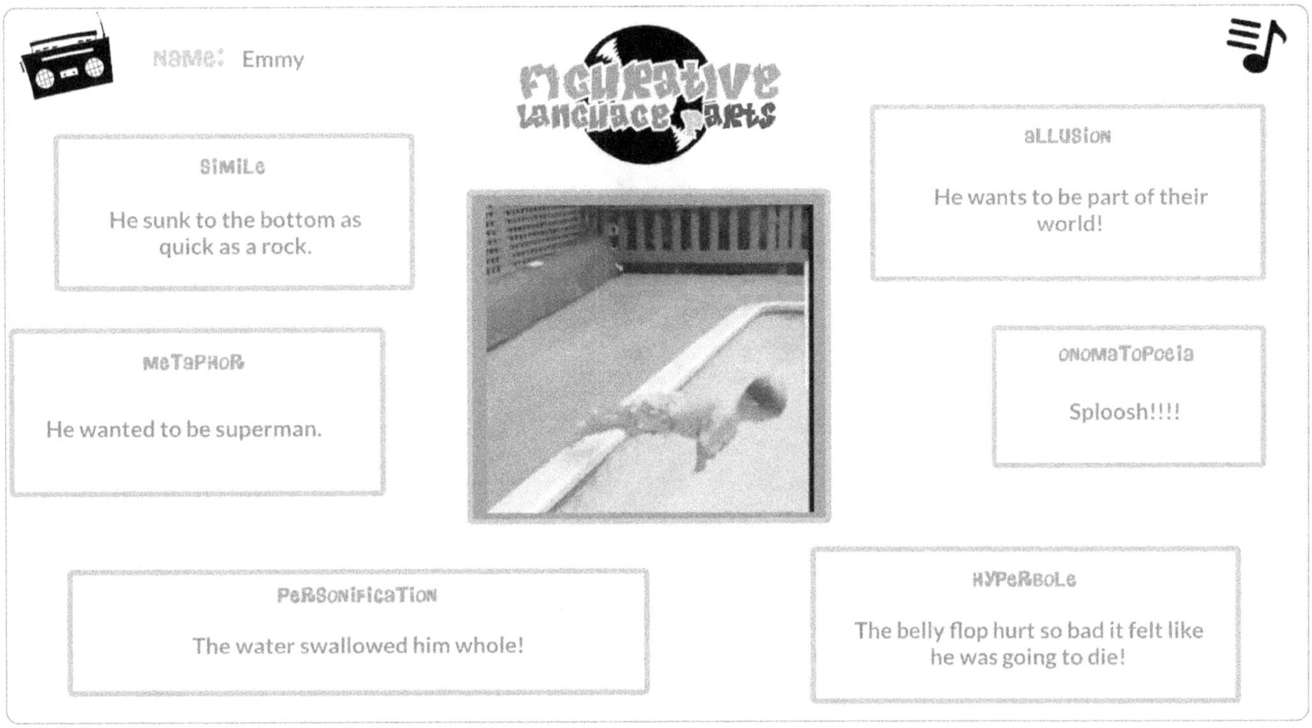

**Name:** Emmy

**Figurative Language Parts**

**Simile**
He sunk to the bottom as quick as a rock.

**Allusion**
He wants to be part of their world!

**Metaphor**
He wanted to be superman.

**Onomatopoeia**
Sploosh!!!!

**Personification**
The water swallowed him whole!

**Hyperbole**
The belly flop hurt so bad it felt like he was going to die!

Wordplay Factory Student Sample

As students gained confidence, I began incorporating images directly related to our content areas, hoping to create natural connections between figurative language and our broader learning goals. Would this protocol still work? My experience with EduProtocols had taught me to trust in the power of repetition and student discovery. The results were both simple and quite encouraging. Students either quickly grasped the different types or collaborated to help each other understand, creating a natural peer learning environment. What used to be six weeks of sequential instruction was now a few short reps.

**Marlena**

Prep time? Mark just needs to download five memes or GIFs or Instagram clips and he's planned for the week. Bonus tip: Give kids points for suggesting things (and making the answer key), and you'll cut your workload even more!

   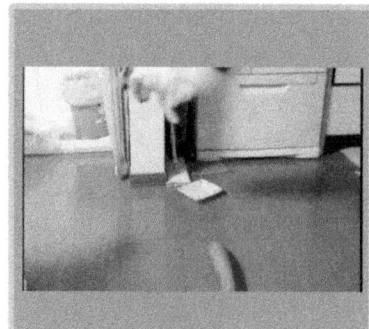

Name: Clara

**Simile**
The cat jumps like it is on a trampoline.

**Metaphor**
The cat is lightning getting shocked.

**Personification**
The floor pushes the cat towards the sky.

**Allusion**
Did the cat eat a poisonous apple?

**Onomatopoeia**
Meow!!

**Hyperbole**
The cat jumped a thousand feet tall.

Wordplay Factory Student Sample #2

## Icon and Template Design

Whenever I have taught figurative language, I have tried to help students see beyond poetry or fiction writing. While these are the traditional areas of focus, I wanted students to see how figurative language is all around them—in music lyrics, hip-hop, movie quotes, and even sports commentary. After all, "Life is like a box of chocolates," right?

When designing and naming this protocol, I decided to elevate the hip-hop vibe. I wanted to build on the playfulness of the Retell in Rhyme EduProtocol but focus on figurative language. I had settled on Figurative Language ARTS but ultimately decided to go more playful. Wordplay kept coming back to my mind, and ultimately, I wanted to have the feel of a playground or lab to play with words. Wordplay Factory was born.

Initial Name and Design

Final Name and Icon Design

The template continued to simplify over time. I wanted this one to feel a little more abstract and loose, like the messy process of writing a song.

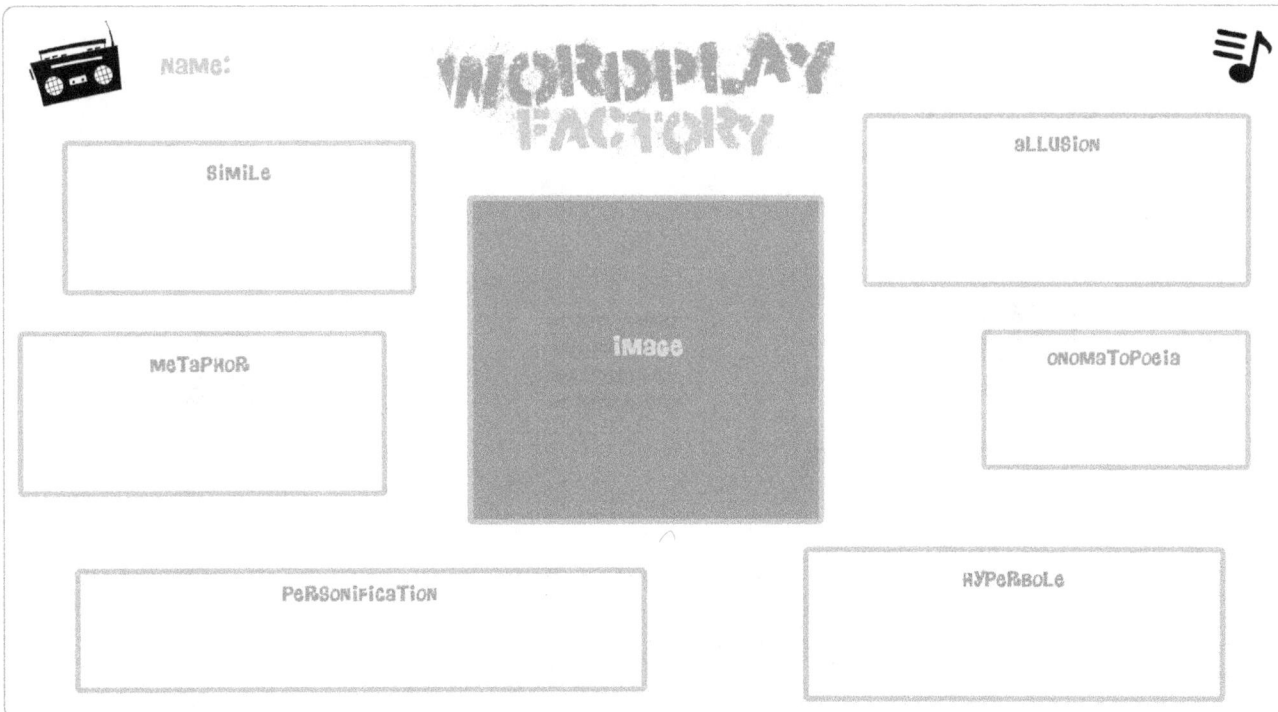

Wordplay Factory Template

## Academic Goals

Through successful implementation of Wordplay Factory, students should:

- Master recognition and creation of multiple types of figurative language.
- Develop confidence in creative language use.
- Transfer figurative language skills to their own writing.
- Connect creative language use to content learning.

## Teacher Big Ideas

- Value creative expression over perfect understanding.
- Use visual prompts to spark imagination.
- Encourage peer teaching and learning.
- Build confidence through regular practice.
- Connect figurative language to real-world content.

One image or source      6 examples of figurative language      Share out in small group

**KEY IDEA:** Students share their single favorite example rather than all. Figurative language is a creative risk, and kids can feel like a few of their examples are "lame." Have them pick one to elevate!

Wordplay Factory Recipe Card

## Prepare for the Activity

1. Select engaging visual prompts (both playful and content-related).
2. Use or modify the template for recording different types of figurative language.
3. Set up Flippity or another random selection tool.
4. Plan for quick, engaging share-outs.

## Instructions

1. Present an engaging visual prompt to the class.
2. Review the six types of figurative language (simile, metaphor, personification, hyperbole, allusion, onomatopoeia).
3. Give students time to create examples of each type.
4. Encourage collaboration and peer support.
5. Use Flippity to randomly select five to six students to share their favorite examples.
6. Celebrate creative and effective uses of figurative language.

## Key Points to Remember

- Keep the atmosphere playful and creative.
- Allow time for peer collaboration.
- Celebrate unique and imaginative responses.
- Don't overexplain—let students discover.
- Use content-related images to build connections.
- Make sharing quick and engaging.

## Variations

- Figurative Language Challenge: Students create their own visual prompts.

- Cross-Curricular Connection: Apply figurative language to different subject areas.
- Songwriting: Students turn their figurative language examples into song lyrics.

The magic of Wordplay Factory lies in its ability to transform what could be a tedious march through literary devices into a dynamic exploration of creative language. When students can craft metaphors and personification for a silly GIF and transfer those same skills to describe scientific processes or historical events, figurative language becomes both accessible and meaningful.

## Your Turn

Wordplay Factory challenges the traditional sequence-based teaching approach by presenting multiple concepts simultaneously. What other sequenced curriculum might benefit from this integrated design approach? Consider how you might create a visual framework that allows students to explore multiple related concepts at once. How would repetition build mastery in your design? What simple visual elements could enhance understanding?

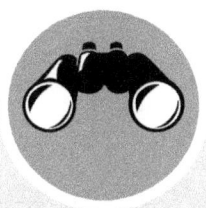

# Chapter 12
## BioBytes EduProtocol

This slide deck includes BioBytes recipe cards, templates, Smart Starts and student samples.

**B**ioBytes shifts traditional biography study into an engaging, repeatable digital experience that emphasizes content mastery while incorporating creative elements and meaningful feedback loops. This protocol streamlines biography analysis by combining essential biographical elements, visual components, and creative interpretation on a single, focused slide, allowing students to develop deeper understanding through multiple iterations across different historical figures.

## Design Story

Like many teachers, I had spent years teaching biography units using traditional methods. Early on, I simply had kids read biographies and answer questions about the person they read about. This evolved into having students create biography boxes out of construction paper. While students enjoyed the crafting aspect, I noticed that too much classroom time was being consumed by the mechanics of folding paper and applying glue, and the focus and quality of information was pretty far from insightful.

Seeking to emphasize content over craft, I transitioned to using Google Forms and increasing repetition. Students would complete a structured questionnaire for each biography they read, addressing areas such as childhood, key events, major accomplishments, life lessons, and famous quotes. This approach provided students with a consistent lens through which to analyze biographical texts, but it lacked engaging feedback loops and creative opportunities for student expression.

> **Marlena**
>
> BioBytes would pair nicely with the Mini-Report, the Research EduProtocol, or Number Mania from *The EduProtocol Field Guide: Book 2* by Marlena Hebern and Jon Corippo.

## Design Iterations

The first iteration of BioBytes brought all these essential biographical elements together on a single slide, creating a more focused and efficient learning experience. However, I soon recognized that students needed additional context to fully appreciate the historical figures they were studying. This led to the addition of a simple timeline component, which not only helped students understand when events occurred but also enabled them to make meaningful comparisons between different historical figures.

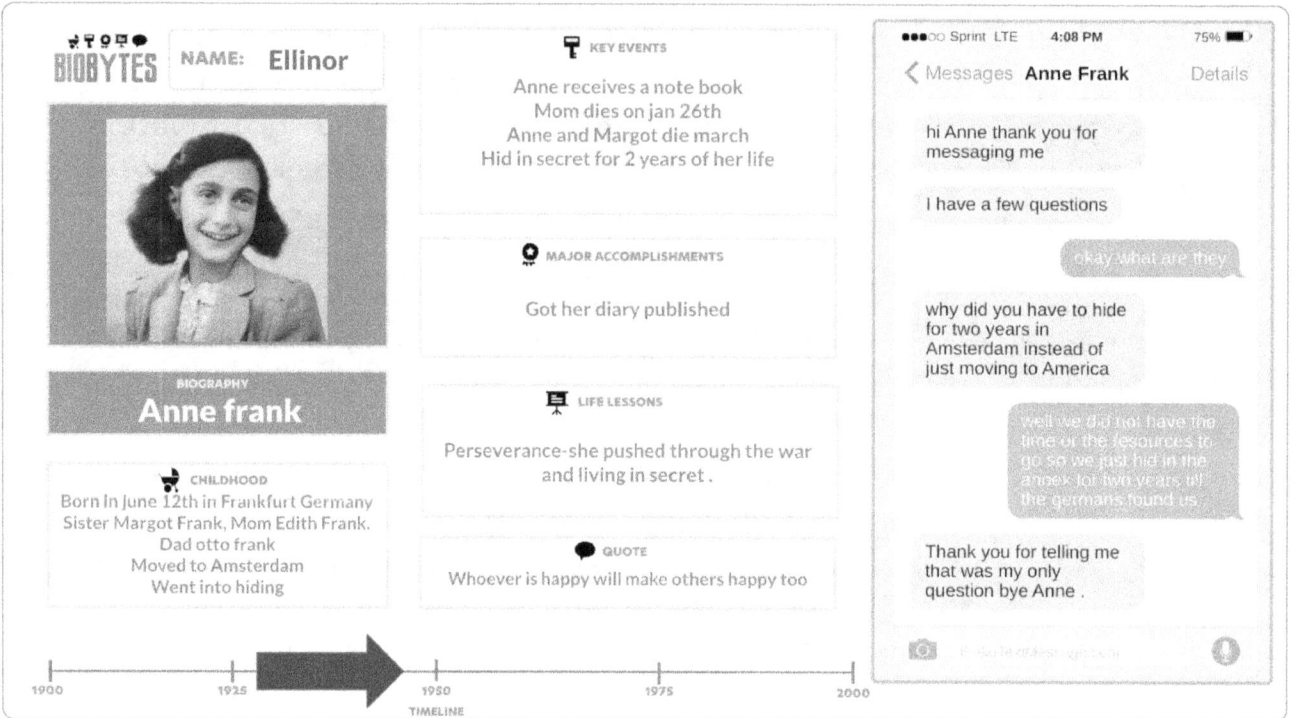

BioBytes Student Sample #1

The next iteration incorporated a visual element (which can even be a primary source), allowing students to include relevant images that enhanced their understanding and connection to the subject. It still needed a creative spark to provide student voice and creativity. The final iteration came with the integration of the dialogue box from the Echo Chamber EduProtocol. This incorporated creative "interviews" with the biographical subjects, adding a layer of engagement and deeper understanding through imaginative interaction.

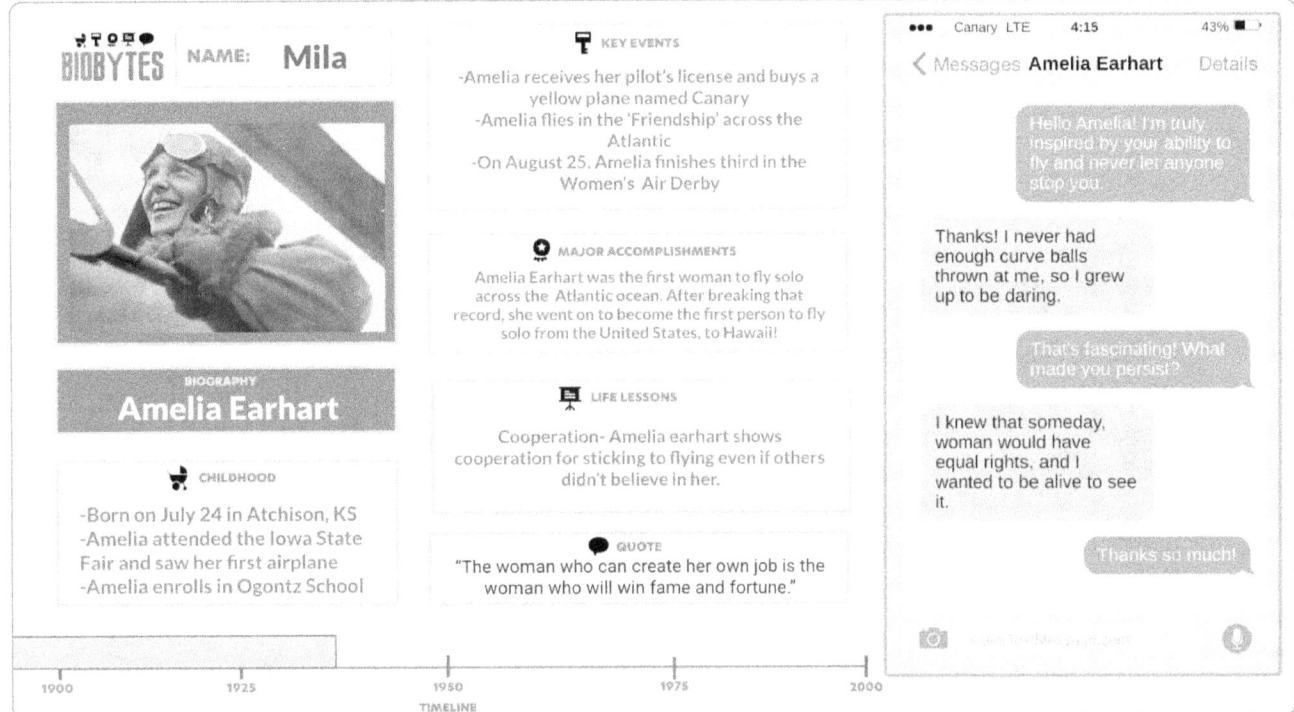

BioBytes Student Sample #2

## Icon and Template Design

This name came pretty quickly. My earlier project was called a BioBox. As I was looking to combine these units of information into one EduProtocol, I started with Biography pARTS. A little while later, it made sense that these units became "bytes," and BioBytes came to be! The icon design holds the five key elements as a reminder to students of what to look for when reading biographies.

I redesigned this template many, many times. It was just a lot of info to squeeze into one slide, so keeping it from being overly busy was a challenge.

**Marlena**

BioBytes is a descriptive name that is also memorable and fun. Mark arrived at this after evolving the name until it made sense and resonated with his students.

Final Name and Icon Design

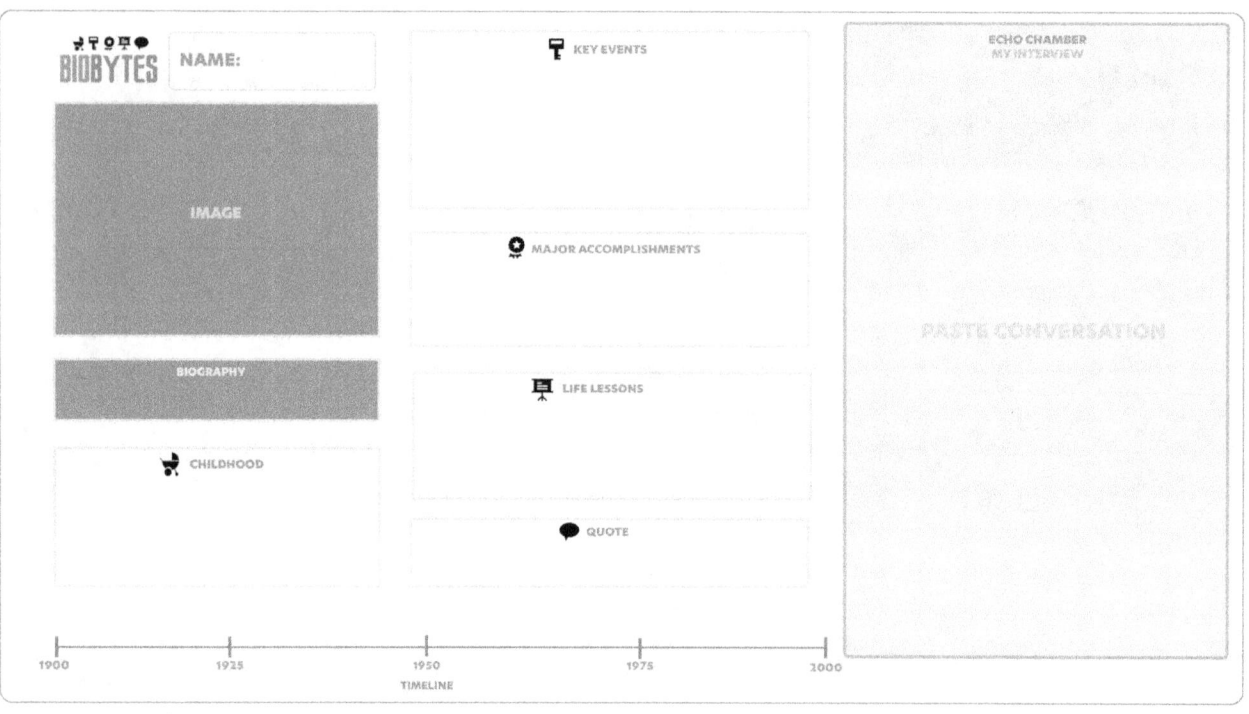

BioBytes Template

## Academic Goals

Through successful implementation of BioBytes, students should:

- Master the key elements of biographical analysis.
- Develop chronological understanding through timeline creation.
- Make connections between historical figures across different time periods.

- Practice creative interpretation through simulated interviews.
- Build skills in identifying and analyzing life lessons from historical figures.

## Teacher Big Ideas

- Prioritize content mastery over decorative elements.
- Create opportunities for multiple repetitions with different subjects.
- Balance structured analysis with creative expression.
- Foster connections between historical figures.
- Build in natural feedback loops through peer sharing.

**Jon**

Being able to do BioBytes all year long will really set kids up for report writing and preps them for quick success in Mini-Reports!

 +  +  +

Read a biography | Capture biographical elements | Generate a fictional dialogue | Share in small groups

**PRO TIP:** Sharing the dialogue box, and then giving them an opportunity to share the "why" behind it, reveals a lot about student understanding.

BioBytes Recipe Card

## Prepare for the Activity

1. Select appropriate biographical texts for your students.
2. Use or modify the template slide, incorporating all elements:
   a. Biographical fact sections (childhood, key events, major accomplishments, life lessons, and famous quotes)
   b. Timeline component
   c. Images
   d. Echo Chamber dialogue box
3. Prepare example slides to model expectations.
4. Plan for sharing and discussion opportunities.

## Instructions

1. Introduce students to the BioBytes template.
2. Model completion of each component using a familiar biographical figure.
3. Guide students through their first biography analysis.
4. Demonstrate effective use of the Echo Chamber dialogue feature.
5. Facilitate sharing sessions to compare different historical figures.
6. Encourage students to identify patterns and connections across biographies.

## Key Points to Remember

- Maintain focus on biographical content over design elements.
- Guide students in selecting meaningful images.
- Foster creative but historically accurate dialogue in the Echo Chamber.

- Create opportunities for students to compare different historical figures.
- Use feedback loops to deepen understanding.

## Variations

- Theme-Based Collection: Group biographies by field, era, or impact.
- Cross-Curricular Connection: Apply BioBytes to historical figures from science, literature, or other content areas.
- Contemporary Connection: Compare historical figures to modern counterparts.
- Collaborative Analysis: Students work in pairs or small groups to complete BioBytes.
- Interview Performance: Act out Echo Chamber dialogues for deeper engagement.
- Archetype Four Square: Incorporate the Archetype Four Square EduProtocol with BioBytes.

The power of BioBytes lies in its ability to combine structured biographical analysis with creative expression while maintaining a clear focus on content mastery. When students can efficiently analyze multiple biographies, make meaningful connections across historical periods, and engage in creative interpretation through simulated interviews, BioBytes becomes an effective approach to biography study that goes beyond traditional craft-based projects.

### Your Turn

BioBytes evolved from traditional projects to a streamlined, content-focused framework. What project-based learning experience in your curriculum spends too much time on mechanics rather than content mastery? How might you redesign it as an EduProtocol that maintains creativity while focusing on essential learning? What elements would you keep, what would you remove, and what new components might enhance learning without adding complexity?

# Chapter 13
# FlipSwitch EduProtocol

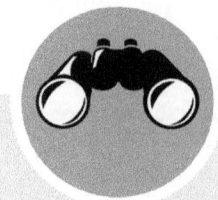

**F**lipSwitch helps students transform problem-focused thinking into action-oriented solutions by teaching them to articulate challenges, define clear outcomes, and identify immediate next steps. This protocol builds executive function skills through repeated practice while making the thinking process both visible and engaging.

This slide deck includes FlipSwitch recipe cards, templates, Smart Starts and student samples.

## Design Story

A pattern I continue to notice in young people is how often they get stuck in problem-focused thinking. They describe their challenges—homework overwhelm, social conflicts, family responsibilities—but struggle to move toward solutions. They need a process to transform these daily challenges into clear outcomes and concrete actions.

One of the core principles of the Getting Things Done methodology is distinguishing between *projects* (outcomes requiring multiple steps) and *next actions* (single, physical steps you can take immediately). Students often confuse these two, which leads directly to procrastination. When a student says "write paper" or "finish project," they're naming an outcome—something that will require multiple actions to complete. But our brains can't *do* outcomes; we can only do actions. The actual next action might be "open Google Docs" or "email teacher to clarify the prompt" or "get notebook from backpack." Until students identify that concrete, physical next step, they often remain stuck.

With GTD, we practice transforming vague "stuff"—all the unprocessed inputs swirling in our heads—into clear outcomes (what "done" looks like) and specific next actions (the single, physical step that moves us forward). Students who develop this habit become unstuck quickly because they know how to break down overwhelming challenges into manageable steps.

This planning challenge raised a question: What if I could take my knowledge and experience with teaching GTD, and my growing practice of designing EduProtocols, and create a protocol that helped students build that muscle of transforming challenges into outcomes and actions?

## Design Iterations

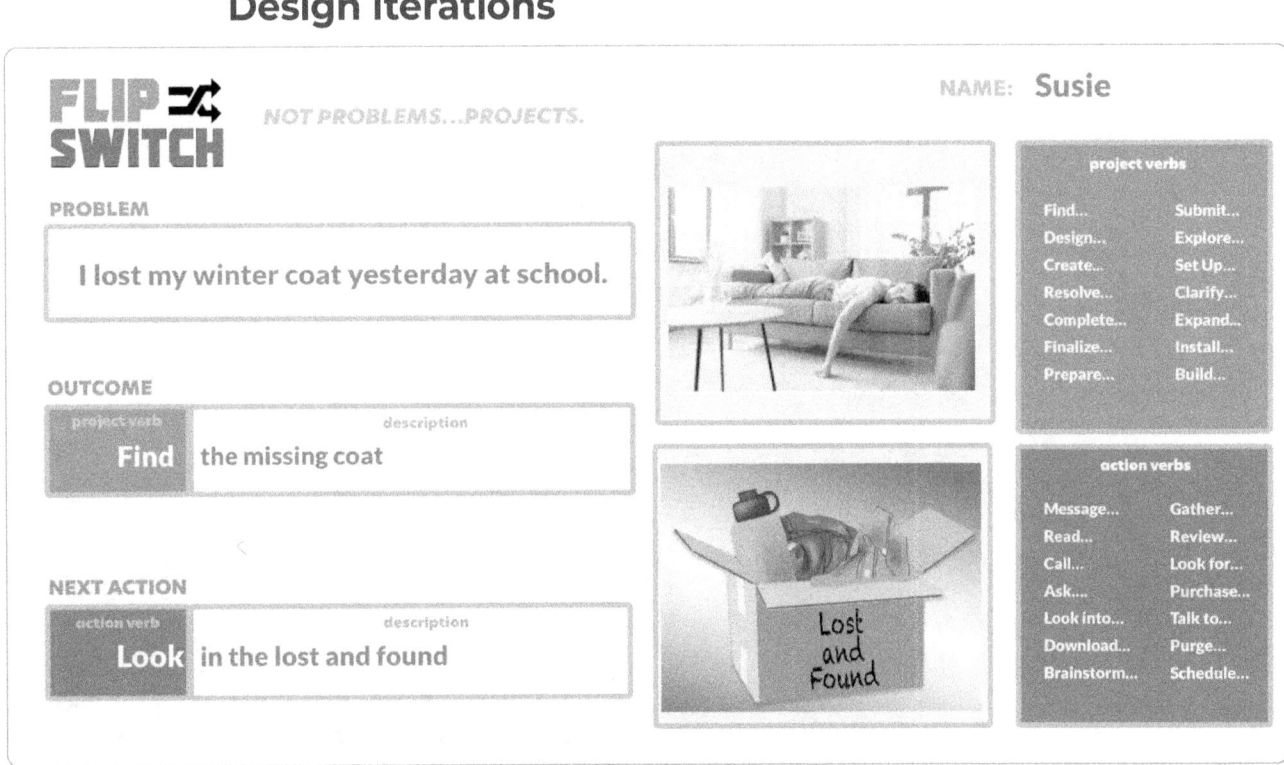

FlipSwitch Student Sample #1

The initial concept for FlipSwitch was straightforward: I created a simple template to help students shift their focus from problems to outcomes. In the first iteration, I presented students with a common issue, then directed them to brainstorm an outcome (finish line) and action to take toward that outcome. I provided a bank of project verbs (describing outcomes that typically require more than one action) and action verbs (describing actions that can typically be executed immediately). This helped, but I still found that discerning the single next action was an ongoing challenge for students.

The early iterations also felt too dry and didn't hit all the EduProtocol criteria. While the methodology was sound, it wasn't fully connecting with youth culture or creating the engagement I was seeing with other EduProtocols. The breakthrough came when I realized FlipSwitch needed to bridge the gap between abstract productivity concepts and concrete student action—helping students articulate the problem they're facing, the desired outcome (what "done" looks like), and most critically, the single, physical next action they can take immediately. But how could I make this visible and engaging?

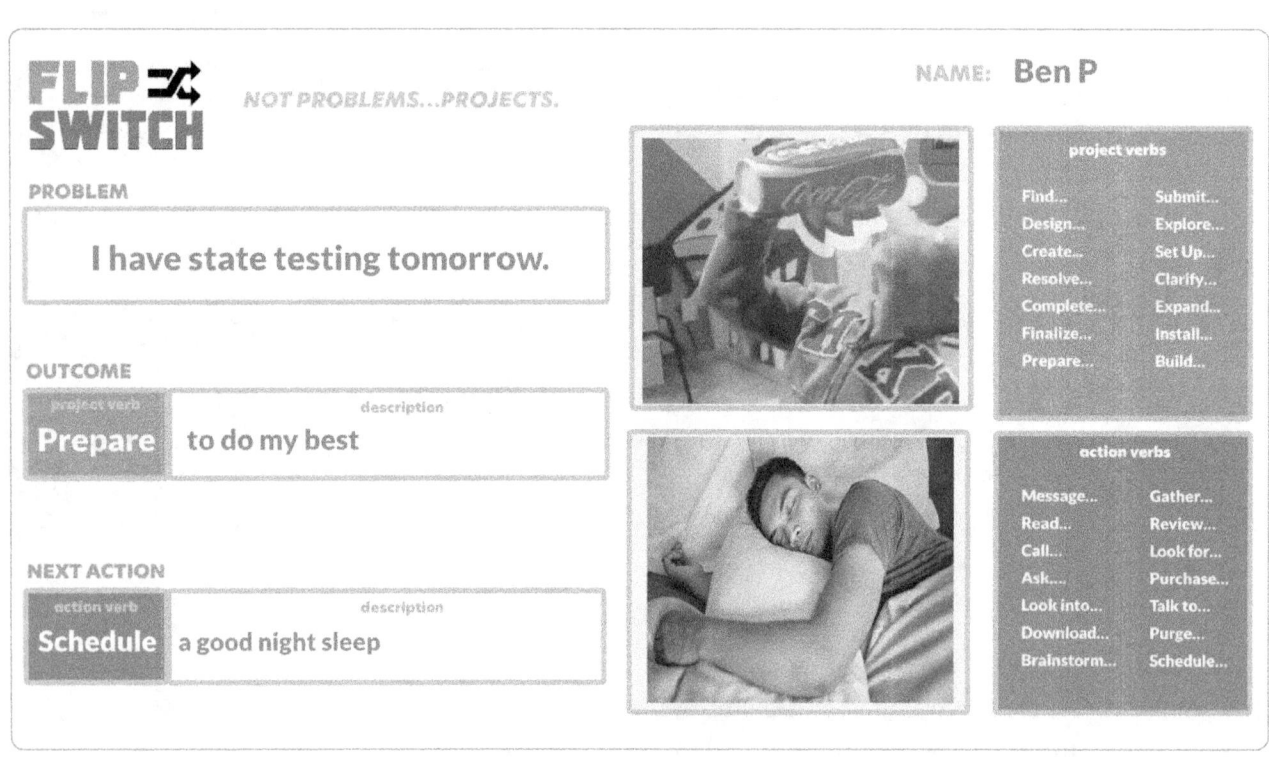

FlipSwitch Student Sample #2

I needed students to think about what a next action would physically look like. So, I had them add an image or GIF of it. This visualization helped students think through the verb associated with getting started. For example, instead of "finish paper," they would get to "turn on Chromebook" or "open backpack." Instead of "finish project," they would get to "buy trifold board" or "ask Mom where the glue is."

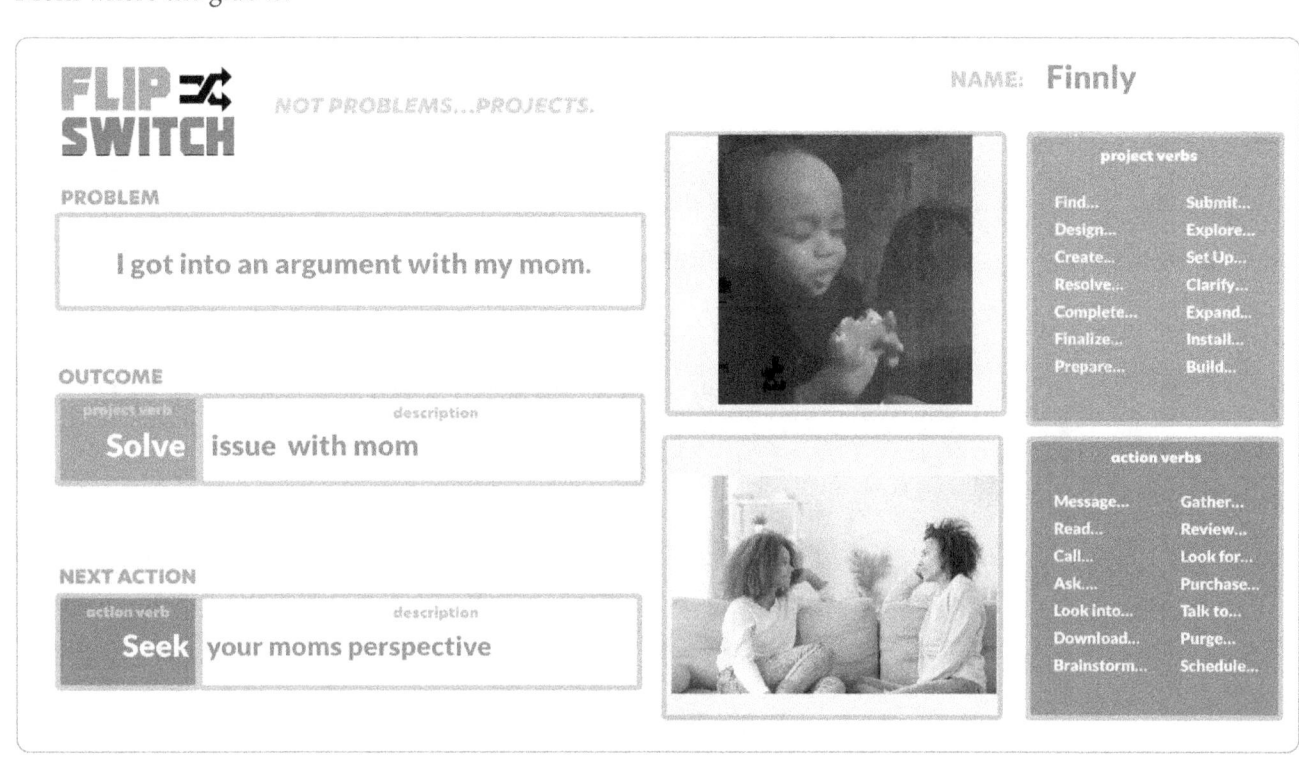

FlipSwitch Student Sample #3

Last, I wanted to add some humor and creativity to FlipSwitch. So often, when I find students stuck in the classroom, they are doing something random and unhelpful. For example, I might find a student doodling on the table or fiddling with a classroom object. When I ask them why they aren't getting started, they reply with something like "I can't find my paper" or "I don't know what to do." To me, the next action seems obvious—go look for your paper or ask a question! But students feel stuck, literally paralyzed, and what they choose to do instead is often comical. So, instead of shaming the kids for these choices, I decided to add some humor to the protocol. Not only do students add an image or GIF of what an effective next action would look like, but the next iteration tasks them to add an image or GIF of what an unhelpful choice would look like.

This. Was. Hilarious. Students started adding GIFs of kids spinning in their chairs, staring out the window, pretending to be a chicken. This added the creativity and levity that was needed. It also provided fodder for the next time situations came up in class. I could identify a choice as being "unhelpful" and ask kids to "flip" it into an effective next action. FlipSwitch was finally coming to life!

To incorporate feedback loops, kids share in pairs or a whole group and see if peers can identify what the next action should be using only the image or GIF. This reiterates the idea that a next action is physical and visible.

Through this iterative process, the protocol became a tool for building executive function skills through repeated practice, helping students develop the habit of breaking down complexity into clarity—a skill that transfers far beyond any single assignment or challenge. Rather than leaving students paralyzed by vague goals like "do better in school," FlipSwitch forces specificity: What does "better" mean? What's one concrete action you can take right now?

## Icon and Template Design

This name was fun. I had so many I liked! I just kept fiddling, playing with words like *action* and *transform*. I liked the word *flip* because it implied that there was another, more positive side to any challenge or problem. I also wanted students to see that they could "switch" their mindset from problems to opportunities. FlipSwitch encompassed that change.

**Mark**

Those ridiculous "unhelpful action" GIFs gave us permission to acknowledge avoidance without judgment. When students aren't defending their choices, they're free to change them.

Final Name and Icon Design

The icon was simple, and the two intertwined arrows capture that sense of action opportunity well. The arrows pointing in opposite directions visualize the core concept—flipping from one state (stuck/problem-focused) to another (action-oriented/solution-focused)—while the bold contrast between blue "FLIP" and gray "SWITCH" emphasizes the transformation process.

The template took a few iterations as I struggled to create a clear visual hierarchy that would guide students through the thinking process without overwhelming them. Because choosing the project verb and action verb were so critical, I contrasted and color-coded them—bright blue for project verbs and dark gray for action verbs—to give these elements more emphasis and weight, helping students quickly distinguish between outcomes they're working toward and immediate actions they can take.

**Mark**

Getting Things Done meets EduProtocol design—when your personal productivity system becomes a student empowerment tool, you know you've found your teaching sweet spot.

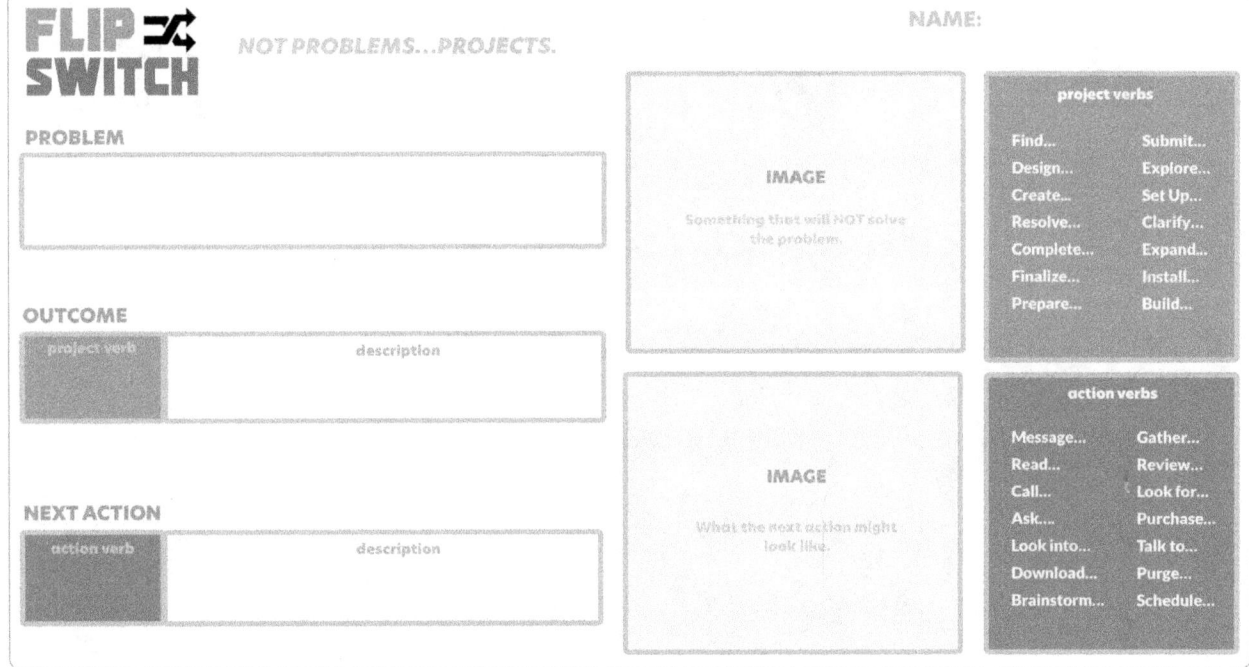

FlipSwitch Template

## Academic Goals

Through successful implementation of FlipSwitch, students should:

- Transform problem statements into outcome statements.
- Identify clear, physical, visible next actions.
- Develop solution-focused thinking habits.
- Build confidence in handling challenges.
- Transfer these skills to various life situations.

 +  +  +

**Present students with a problem or scenario** — **Identify a desired outcome and next action** — **Add visuals of what action would and would not look like** — **Share out in small group**

**PRO TIP:** Help students differentiate between outcomes and actions using the verb banks.

FlipSwitch Recipe Card

## Teacher Big Ideas

- Keep it quick and energetic.
- Embrace both real and scenario-based problems.
- Celebrate creative transformations.
- Connect to student experiences.

## Prepare for the Activity

1. Provide a template for your students.
2. Prepare mix of scenarios and real situations.
3. Plan for quick sharing and feedback.

## Instructions

1. Present situation (personal or scenario).
2. Guide the "flip" from problem to outcome.
3. Identify next physical action.
4. Build on successes through repetition.

## Key Points to Remember

- Maintain a fast pace.
- Build psychological safety.
- Connect to real student experiences.

## Variations

- Subject-Specific: Apply to academic challenges.
- Social Focus: Address relationship situations.
- Future Planning: Target academic/future goals.
- Team Challenge: Engage in collaborative problem-solving.

The power of FlipSwitch lies in its simplicity and immediate applicability. When students transform overload into clear outcomes and identify next actions, they experience the power of transforming "stuff." When they see peers making similar transformations, they build confidence in their own ability to handle challenges.

## Your Turn

FlipSwitch demonstrates how executive function challenges can be transformed into engaging learning opportunities through EduProtocol design. Consider an area of executive function where your students struggle. How might you create an EduProtocol that helps them practice the type of thinking you are hoping for? What youth culture elements (like GIFs or memes) might you incorporate to make your protocol both effective and engaging? Remember that small shifts in how we frame challenges—like adding humor to FlipSwitch—can transform student engagement.

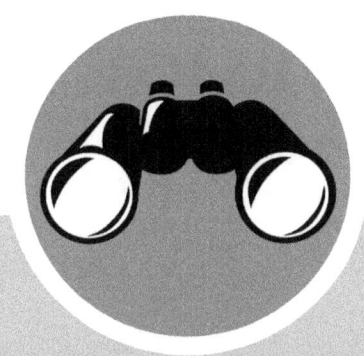

# SECTION 3
## Designing Your Own EduProtocols

# Chapter 14
## Designing Your Own EduProtocols

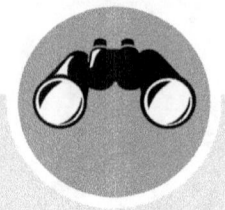

**Look for red cars, and suddenly you notice red cars everywhere.** They were always there, but you alerted your brain and tuned your attention to them. I experienced that same shift when I began thinking about teaching through the lens of EduProtocols; I noticed opportunities to design EduProtocols everywhere. Have some vocabulary to learn? Reach for Fast and Curious. Need to engage multiple perspectives? Bring in 3x POV. Even now, as I hear about new curricula, I'm scanning for repetition, for immediate feedback loops, for sizzle, for opportunity.

Every teacher is a designer. This isn't hyperbole—it's simply the nature of teaching. When you craft lesson plans, you're designing learning experiences. When you arrange your physical classroom for better discussions, you're designing spaces. When you adjust your teaching mid-lesson because students aren't quite connecting with the material, you're engaging in real-time design iteration.

The process of creating EduProtocols builds naturally on the design skills you already use every day. Making the leap to designing EduProtocols is simply about looking at your teaching practice through a new lens, much like looking for red cars. The opportunities for EduProtocol design have always existed in your classroom. My hope is that through this book, you'll start seeing them more clearly and have the confidence to take the risk of stepping into the beautiful, fulfilling messiness of designing your own.

Consider your current daily teaching cycle. You begin with establishing outcomes, then brainstorm approaches to achieve them, implement your ideas, gather feedback through student responses, and adjust your approach accordingly. This cycle of design, implement, reflect, and refine isn't just teaching—it's design thinking in action. Creating EduProtocols simply channels this thinking into the form of repeatable frameworks that can work across multiple contexts.

Implementing and then designing EduProtocols well might initially take some energy, thought, and creativity, adding more to your already heavy workload. But only at first. Ultimately, you'll learn to seek opportunities to streamline and simplify your teaching while also deepening student engagement. This is a win/win prospect for you and your students.

## Where to Look for EduProtocol Opportunities

Let's examine where your current teaching practices might already be inviting EduProtocol design.

### Standards Integration

Look for natural connections between standards you're currently teaching separately. Reading comprehension might pair with writing and speaking skills. Scientific observation could combine with technical writing. These types of connections and overlap can create richer learning experiences while also maximizing instructional time.

In my own practice, I discovered that teaching capitalization rules separately from writing instruction was inefficient—students could pass grammar quizzes but still failed to capitalize correctly in their actual writing. By integrating capitalization practice directly into writing revision through the Capitalization pARTS protocol, students applied the rules in authentic contexts while simultaneously developing editing skills, saving instructional time and improving transfer of learning.

### Youth Culture Connection

Pay attention to what engages your students outside of school. Their social media habits might inform how you structure peer feedback. Their gaming interests might inspire the timing of activities or other gamified structures. Your students are constantly showing you what captures their attention—use these insights in your design.

Students who spend hours perfecting their gaming strategies understand concepts like leveling up, immediate feedback, and iterative improvement—all principles that translate directly to effective learning design. Rather than fighting against gaming culture, consider how timed challenges, visible progress indicators, or collaborative problem-solving structures from games could inform your protocol design, making academic work feel as engaging as the activities students voluntarily pursue outside school.

## Repeated Practice

Identify areas where students need regular practice opportunities. Design protocols that allow for repeated skill development that will not feel repetitive. Consider how popular apps and games maintain engagement through multiple iterations, then apply these principles to your protocols.

## Feedback Loops

Immediate feedback is a critical element of effective learning. However, feedback does not need to come from the teacher alone. Look for alternative ways for students to receive feedback on their learning, from whole-group sessions to peers to AI. Just make sure it's timely. Stop grading over the weekend. By Monday, your students won't really care. It's too late.

In Word Hunters, students present their mystery word clues to classmates who have three chances to guess the answer, creating immediate peer feedback that happens within the same lesson rather than days later when the learning moment has passed. Similarly, using shared slide decks where students can see each other's work in real time—whether it's StoryScan book analyses or Thin Slides presentations—transforms feedback from a delayed, teacher-only event into an ongoing conversation where students learn from multiple perspectives while their thinking is still fresh and malleable.

## The Design Process

Starting your first EduProtocol doesn't require reinventing the wheel or blinding inspiration. Begin with an activity or teaching strategy that already works well in your classroom. Ask yourself:

1. Could this work with different content?
2. How might it incorporate multiple standards?
3. Where could feedback loops enhance learning?
4. What elements of youth culture could make it more engaging?
5. What time constraints create better structure?
6. How can I infuse student choice and creativity?

## When Things Don't Go as Planned

Remember that iteration is part of design. When your protocol takes unexpected turns:

- Observe what actually happened versus what you expected.
- Consider whether the "failure" might reveal a better approach.
- Make adjustments based on classroom evidence.
- Try again, knowing each iteration improves the design.

## Sizzle: Naming and Icon Design

Embrace the tension of sizzle. Don't decorate trash with beauty. Don't decorate beauty with trash. With EduProtocols, you are not trying to make boring activities appear fun by calling them cute names or adding pretty colors. This will be sniffed out by students, and you will lose credibility quickly.

**Jon**

I have found that when I give immediate feedback, students grow immediately. You also give yourself the gift of the night (or weekend) off.

**Marlena**

Standards, youth culture connection, repeated practice, and feedback loops will help you see the "red cars" of EduProtocol opportunity in your classroom!

**Mark**

Designing can be unpredictable and messy. Seek to be *comfortable being uncomfortable*. The reality is that our teaching practice is always in beta!

**Jon**

Keep early efforts quick, like 5–8 minutes, and do new things at the end of a period. This way you can do 3–4 practice reps without impacting your flow and if it all goes badly, you can say: "There's the bell!"

> **Jon**
> Don't rush the name; let it take its own time.

> **Jon**
> We don't design EduProtocols for a single book or unit. They should transcend subject matter whenever possible. This means we don't have a lesson for *The Giver*, for example. We have EduProtocols for reading comprehension. And they might work for history and science as well.

That said, creating novelty and cognitive categories for students can enhance learning. Design means something to the brain; it brings order out of chaos and meaning out of mess. Spend time and be thoughtful about how you name and design your EduProtocol. This thought further enhances your intentionality.

The name FlipSwitch emerged after considering dozens of alternatives. I knew the name needed to capture both the transformation (flip) and the empowerment to change direction (switch), while the intertwined arrows in the icon visually reinforced this concept of redirecting from being stuck to moving forward. Similarly, Word Hunters immediately communicates active searching and discovery rather than passive vocabulary memorization.

## Moving Forward

When you begin designing EduProtocols, start small. Look for one area where a repeatable protocol might streamline your teaching while deepening student engagement. Perhaps it's a reading strategy that could work across multiple texts. Maybe it's a discussion format that could apply to different content areas.

Remember that your existing teaching wisdom is the foundation for EduProtocol design. Every adjustment you've made to a lesson plan, every modification to meet student needs, every creative solution to a classroom challenge has developed your design expertise.

The pathway to creating effective EduProtocols isn't about learning an entirely new skill set—it's about channeling your existing design capabilities in a new direction. As you begin noticing these opportunities in your classroom, remember that each small step in EduProtocol design has the potential to create powerful learning experiences for your students.

## Your Turn

Now that you've seen the design journey for multiple EduProtocols, identify one teaching challenge you face regularly that might benefit from a protocol approach. Draft a simple framework addressing this challenge, incorporating the following:

- Multiple standards
- At least two feedback loops
- Elements of youth culture
- Potential for repetition

Remember, your first design doesn't need to be perfect—it just needs to start the iterative process that leads to powerful learning experiences.

# Chapter 15
## Join the Movement:
## Become the Designer You Already Are

**Teaching can feel isolating, but you're not alone in this journey.** Across the globe, there is a growing community of educators engaged with EduProtocols. I had the opportunity to attend an EduProtocols Summer Academy in Laguna Beach, and I saw the collective impact of EduProtocols; I felt the synergy and excitement. EduProtocols have inspired an online Facebook community of nearly twenty-five thousand educators looking to grow together, support each other, and push the envelope of teaching and learning. This community is sharing ideas, iterating designs, and supporting each other's growth. This isn't traditional professional development; it's something far more powerful—teachers learning from teachers, growing together, and changing education one EduProtocol at a time.

Now it's your turn to join this movement.

## From Reader to Designer

You've read about what makes an EduProtocol tick. You explored the basic principles of design. You've seen that, as a teacher, you're already a designer in countless ways. Perhaps you're already seeing potential EduProtocols everywhere (those red cars are hard to unsee, aren't they?). Maybe you've even started sketching out ideas for your own EduProtocol.

Here's where it gets really exciting. We want you, the reader, to become a part of the EduProtocol design team.

At the end of this book, you'll see a QR code. This is an invitation, a gateway to becoming a deeper part of the EduProtocol multiverse.

When you scan the QR code, you will be redirected to an EduProtocol submission form. As you walk the path of EduProtocol design, we are confident that you will unlock something beautifully creative. Something that could inspire other educators, engage other students, and enhance the EduProtocol community. The best new EduProtocols are not in this book or the next. The best new EduProtocols are out in this community, in the readers of this book, just waiting to take form and be unleashed.

**Marlena**

*All* of the EduProtocols have been created by educators just like you! We cannot wait to see what you create! Share with us? Yes, indeed!

## What We're Looking For

When you're ready to share your EduProtocol with others, don't worry or be intimidated—we're not looking for perfection. Some of the most powerful EduProtocols started out looking rather humble. What matters is the core design, the engagement factor, the potential for impact.

The submission form will guide you through some reflective questions based on the criteria we explored in chapter 4. This helps ensure you're creating an EduProtocol rather than a one-off activity. Remember, we're looking for protocols that:

- Combine multiple standards.
- Create authentic feedback loops.
- Tap into youth culture.
- Work across content areas.
- Support repetition and growth.

Your initial design doesn't need to be visually perfect. That sleek, polished look can come later. Some of the most effective EduProtocols look decidedly unglamorous, but their core design is gold. The visual elements tend to evolve or simplify over time—the community often helps with that.

**Marlena**

Simplicity is beautiful and allows for optimal student creativity!

## The Jedi Council Review Process

Once you submit your design, your proposed EduProtocol will go before what we playfully call the Jedi Council (yes, we're embracing our inner nerds here). Led by EduProtocol creators Jon Corippo and Marlena Hebern, along with a team of other OG EduProtocol designers, this group of experienced educators will review each submission with care and consideration.

You'll receive one of two responses.

### Response One

You'll receive thoughtful feedback on how to strengthen your protocol's design, helping you refine your EduProtocol for maximum impact.

### Response Two

Your submission will be approved. You will receive a certification graphic declaring your EduProtocol will officially become part of the EduProtocol multiverse!

Submission Process

This certification isn't supposed to serve as a sticker on a worksheet. It's recognition that you've created something valuable, something that can help teachers and students beyond your own classroom. You will be officially recognized as a published EduProtocol designer and receive a badge. You will be credited with the EduProtocol design, and you can proudly display your badge, add it to your email signature, even include it on your résumé.

### Your Impact Beyond Your Classroom

But here's what really matters: Your EduProtocol could become part of something bigger. It joins a growing collection of tools that teachers worldwide can use to engage students, deepen learning, and make education more effective, enjoyable, and sustainable for everyone involved. Your design could help a teacher in Seattle engage struggling readers, support a classroom in Sydney mastering scientific concepts, or transform how students in Singapore approach mathematical thinking.

This is how we change education—not through top-down mandates or isolated innovations but through teachers supporting teachers, sharing ideas and building on each other's creativity.

**Jon**

We are tired of waiting for college professors and publishers to save us. We are going to need to save ourselves through thoughtful practice and collaboration.

## Ready to Take the Next Step?

Ready to move from consumer to creator? Ready to join a movement that's transforming education one protocol at a time?

Remember the mantra:

*Teach Better. Work Less. Achieve More.*

It's not just a tagline. It's a promise. And with your help, it's becoming reality in classrooms around the world.

### Your Turn

As our journey together concludes, what's your next step as an EduProtocol designer? Will you adapt an existing protocol, create something entirely new, or collaborate with colleagues on a shared design? Set a specific design goal with a timeline and identify one person who can provide feedback on your creation. The EduProtocol community grows stronger with each educator who shifts from consumer to creator.

We're excited to see what you'll design!

Your move. Your moment.

Scan that QR code. Join the movement. Let's change education together.

Join the Movement! Submit Your Ideas Here!

**Mark**

That QR code isn't just a submission form—it's an invitation to shift from consumer to creator. The best EduProtocols haven't been invented yet. They're in the minds of the educators reading this book.

# Acknowledgments

This book exists because of a community of educators who believe teaching can be better, more sustainable, and more joyful.

To Jon Corippo and Marlena Hebern: Thank you for creating EduProtocols and for welcoming me into this movement. Your mentorship transformed my teaching practice and gave me permission to design.

To Dave Burgess and the team at Dave Burgess Consulting: Thank you for championing teacher voices and for believing that educators have wisdom worth sharing.

To Matt, my colleague down the hall who wouldn't stop talking about EduProtocols: I'm sorry I dismissed your excitement for so long. You were right. Thank you for your patience and persistence.

To my students, past, present, and future: You are my best teachers. Thank you for your creativity, your honesty when things didn't work, and your willingness to try "just one more rep."

To David Allen: Thank you for your life-changing work and for trusting me to bring GTD to young people.

To Mom and Dad: Thank you for the endless sacrifice and encouragement.

To Todd, my brother: Thank you for introducing me to GTD in 2008. That conversation rippled further than either of us imagined.

To Nikki, my wife: You taught me to see design. More importantly, you've supported every long day, every "what if I tried this," and every moment of doubt. Thank you for being my partner in this beautifully chaotic life of teaching, parenting, and creating.

To my four kids: Thank you for sharing your dad with this work. You remind me every day why education matters and why teachers need sustainable practices. I hope you grow up knowing that work can be meaningful without consuming your life.

To Deb, my teaching partner of twenty-five years: You've been more than a colleague; you've been a mentor, a collaborator, and a friend. This book is dedicated to you because none of my best teaching moments happened without you.

To the 23,000+ educators in the EduProtocol community: You inspire me. Keep designing. Keep sharing. Keep making teaching better for all of us.

And finally, to every teacher reading this: You're already a designer. Thank you for the work you do every single day. May these protocols give you margin, energy, and joy in your practice.

Ever wished you could pick the brains of the EduProtocols pioneers? Now you *can* at EduProtocolsPlus.com!

**One price for a *lifetime* of support!**

- Reusable templates with regular additions
- Exclusive live and recorded shows featuring EduProtocols authors and experts
- Self-paced courses
- Supportive community
- Discounts on events
- District plans available

EduProtocolsPlus.com

## EduProtocols books for teaching and leadership

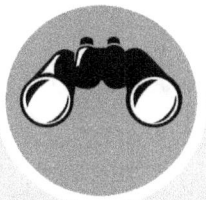

# About Mark Wallace

**Mark B. Wallace** has spent over twenty years teaching in a multiage elementary classroom in the Minneapolis area. He is the coauthor of *Getting Things Done for Teens* (with David Allen and Mike Williams, 2018) and creator of GTD K–12, launched in 2025 to bring Getting Things Done methodology to classrooms across the globe.

As an EduProtocol designer, Mark has created multiple protocols including FlipSwitch, Echo Chamber, BioBytes, StoryScan, and ReRoute. He is known for his visual design work within the EduProtocol community.

Mark is an international speaker and TEDx presenter who specializes in making the complex simple and bringing order out of chaos. His presentations help teachers create sustainable practices that energize both students and educators.

Mark resides in Bloomington, Minnesota, with his wife Nikki and their four children.

# About Marlena Hebern

**Marlena Hebern** is an educator, coach, and co-creator of EduProtocols who loves helping teachers transform learning in ways that are clear, creative, and meaningful. Having spent her career in classrooms and supporting schools across the country, Marlena brings not only expertise but also curiosity, humor, and a genuine love for seeing students light up with understanding. (Truly her favorite!)

She designs and facilitates professional learning that helps teachers focus on meaningful content rather than getting lost in complicated processes. In partnership with EduProtocols Plus, Marlena works alongside educators to implement routines that spark engagement, deepen understanding, and save time.

Known for her practical wisdom and approachable style, Marlena helps educators adapt EduProtocols to meet the needs of different learners, grade levels, and content areas. She bridges research-informed practices with real classroom needs—making instruction both rigorous and understandable, while still leaving room for joy and curiosity.

Marlena lives in Maryland, where she enjoys connecting with fellow educators, tinkering with new teaching tools, and reveling in playful adventures with her two grandchildren—whether that's building epic Brio train worlds, racing cars around the living room, or laughing at how her own over-the-top dance moves impress the toddlers.

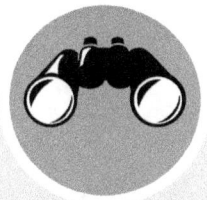

# About Jon Corippo

**Jon Corippo** has been in education for over twenty-five years. He's been a grade 4-8 teacher, taught 9-12 classes in several areas, and has been a high school principal and a county-level assistant superintendent. Jon served at one of California's largest EDU nonprofits as chief learning officer and executive director.

School was not enjoyable for Jon, and now he shares the EduProtocols pedagogical approach to bring dramatically better classroom outcomes for students and teachers. Jon's pedagogical skills were very apparent when he returned to the classroom in 2020-21 (during COVID) and quadrupled his student scores from 9 percent to 41 percent passing in math and doubled student scores in ELA as well. This was at a time most folks were experiencing "learning loss."

Jon's passion project for the last six years has been EduProtocols, which has sold over 80,000 copies globally. Jon has presented to over 100,000 educators and done over 1,000 classroom takeovers in ten states and five countries in the last 3.5 years alone.

Jon is famous for his "free lifetime tech support." He's happy to answer any and all questions at jcorippo@gmail.com or in the EduProtocols community on Facebook.

Jon is only an educator because of his amazing wife. She started the whole project that changed his life. After not once encouraging his kids to be in education, Nolan, Mia, and Claire are all in education-based jobs. Life is funny that way.

Jon lives near Yosemite and spends his free time as the head maintenance person for the family Airbnbs. Yes, there's a teacher discount. Just email him to access it.

# More from Dave Burgess Consulting, Inc.

Since 2012, DBCI has published books that inspire and equip educators to be their best. For more information on our titles or to purchase bulk orders for your school, district, or book study, visit DaveBurgessConsulting.com/DBCIbooks.

## The *Like a PIRATE*™ Series

*Teach Like a PIRATE* by Dave Burgess
*eXPlore Like a PIRATE* by Michael Matera
*Learn Like a PIRATE* by Paul Solarz
*Plan Like a PIRATE* by Dawn M. Harris
*Play Like a PIRATE* by Quinn Rollins
*Run Like a PIRATE* by Adam Welcome
*Tech Like a PIRATE* by Matt Miller

## The *Lead Like a PIRATE*™ Series

*Lead Like a PIRATE* by Shelley Burgess and Beth Houf
*Balance Like a PIRATE* by Jessica Cabeen, Jessica Johnson, and Sarah Johnson
*Lead beyond Your Title* by Nili Bartley
*Lead with Appreciation* by Amber Teamann and Melinda Miller
*Lead with Collaboration* by Allyson Apsey and Jessica Gomez
*Lead with Culture* by Jay Billy
*Lead with Instructional Rounds* by Vicki Wilson
*Lead with Literacy* by Mandy Ellis
*She Leads* by Dr. Rachael George and Majalise W. Tolan

## The EduProtocol® Field Guide Series

*Deploying EduProtocols* by Kim Voge, with Jon Corippo and Marlena Hebern
*The EduProtocol Field Guide* by Marlena Hebern and Jon Corippo
*The EduProtocol Field Guide Book 2* by Marlena Hebern and Jon Corippo
*The EduProtocol Field Guide Math Edition* by Lisa Nowakowski and Jeremiah Ruesch
*The EduProtocol Field Guide Primary Edition* by Benjamin Cogswell and Jennifer Dean
*The EduProtocol Field Guide Social Studies Edition* by Dr. Scott M. Petri and Adam Moler
*The EduProtocol Field Guide ELA Edition* by Jacob Carr

## Leadership & School Culture

*Autopilot* by Rich Czyz
*Be 1% Better* by Ron Clark
*Be THAT Teacher* by Dwayne Reed
*Beyond the Surface of Restorative Practices* by Marisol Rerucha
*Change the Narrative* by Henry J. Turner and Kathy Lopes
*Choosing to See* by Pamela Seda and Kyndall Brown
*Culturize* by Jimmy Casas
*Discipline Win* by Andy Jacks
*Educate Me!* by Dr. Shree Walker with Micheal D. Ison
*Escaping the School Leader's Dunk Tank* by Rebecca Coda and Rick Jetter
*Fight Song* by Kim Bearden
*From Teacher to Leader* by Starr Sackstein
*If the Dance Floor Is Empty, Change the Song* by Joe Clark
*The Innovator's Mindset* by George Couros
*It's OK to Say "They"* by Christy Whittlesey
*Kids Deserve It!* by Todd Nesloney and Adam Welcome
*Leading the Whole Teacher* by Allyson Apsey
*Let Them Speak* by Rebecca Coda and Rick Jetter
*The Limitless School* by Abe Hege and Adam Dovico
*Live Your Excellence* by Jimmy Casas
*Next-Level Teaching* by Jonathan Alsheimer
*The Pepper Effect* by Sean Gaillard
*Principaled* by Kate Barker, Kourtney Ferrua, and Rachael George
*The Principled Principal* by Jeffrey Zoul and Anthony McConnell
*Relentless* by Hamish Brewer
*The Secret Solution* by Todd Whitaker, Sam Miller, and Ryan Donlan
*Start. Right. Now.* by Todd Whitaker, Jeffrey Zoul, and Jimmy Casas
*Stop. Right. Now.* by Jimmy Casas and Jeffrey Zoul
*Teach Your Class Off* by CJ Reynolds
*Teachers Deserve It* by Rae Hughart and Adam Welcome
*They Call Me "Mr. De"* by Frank DeAngelis
*Thrive through the Five* by Jill M. Siler
*Unmapped Potential* by Julie Hasson and Missy Lennard
*When Kids Lead* by Todd Nesloney and Adam Dovico
*Word Shift* by Joy Kirr
*Your School Rocks* by Ryan McLane and Eric Lowe

## Technology & Tools

*50 Things to Go Further with Google Classroom* by Alice Keeler and Libbi Miller
*50 Things You Can Do with Google Classroom* by Alice Keeler and Libbi Miller
*50 Ways to Engage Students with Google Apps* by Alice Keeler and Heather Lyon
*140 Twitter Tips for Educators* by Brad Currie, Billy Krakower, and Scott Rocco
*AI Optimism* by Becky Keene
*Block Breaker* by Brian Aspinall
*Building Blocks for Tiny Techies* by Jamila "Mia" Leonard
*Code Breaker* by Brian Aspinall
*The Complete EdTech Coach* by Katherine Goyette and Adam Juarez
*Control Alt Achieve* by Eric Curts
*The Esports Education Playbook* by Chris Aviles, Steve Isaacs, Christine Lion-Bailey, and Jesse Lubinsky
*Google Apps for Littles* by Christine Pinto and Alice Keeler
*Master the Media* by Julie Smith
*Raising Digital Leaders* by Jennifer Casa-Todd
*Reality Bytes* by Christine Lion-Bailey, Jesse Lubinsky, and Micah Shippee, PhD
*Sail the 7 Cs with Microsoft Education* by Becky Keene and Kathi Kersznowski
*Shake Up Learning* by Kasey Bell
*Social LEADia* by Jennifer Casa-Todd
*Stepping Up to Google Classroom* by Alice Keeler and Kimberly Mattina
*Teaching Math with Google Apps* by Alice Keeler and Diana Herrington
*Teaching with Google Jamboard* by Alice Keeler and Kimberly Mattina
*Teachingland* by Amanda Fox and Mary Ellen Weeks

## Teaching Methods & Materials

*All 4s and 5s* by Andrew Sharos
*Boredom Busters* by Katie Powell
*Building Strong Writers* by Christina Schneider
*The Classroom Chef* by John Stevens and Matt Vaudrey
*The Collaborative Classroom* by Trevor Muir
*Copyrighteous* by Diana Gill
*CREATE* by Bethany J. Petty
*Ditch That Homework* by Matt Miller and Alice Keeler
*Ditch That Textbook* by Matt Miller
*Don't Ditch That Tech* by Matt Miller, Nate Ridgway, and Angelia Ridgway

*EDrenaline Rush* by John Meehan

*Educated by Design* by Michael Cohen, The Tech Rabbi

*Empowered to Choose: A Practical Guide to Personalized Learning* by Andrew Easton

*Expedition Science* by Becky Schnekser

*Frustration Busters* by Katie Powell

*Fully Engaged* by Michael Matera and John Meehan

*Game On? Brain On!* by Lindsay Portnoy, PhD

*Guided Math AMPED* by Reagan Tunstall

*Happy & Resilient* by Roni Habib

*Innovating Play* by Jessica LaBar-Twomy and Christine Pinto

*Instant Relevance* by Denis Sheeran

*Instructional Coaching Connection* by Nathan Lang-Raad

*Keeping the Wonder* by Jenna Copper, Ashley Bible, Abby Gross, and Staci Lamb

*LAUNCH* by John Spencer and A.J. Juliani

*Learning in the Zone* by Dr. Sonny Magana

*Less Talk, More Action* by Allyson Apsey and Emily Freeland

*Lights, Cameras, TEACH!* by Kevin J. Butler

*The Magical CTE Classroom* by Tisha Richmond

*Make Learning MAGICAL* by Tisha Richmond

*Pass the Baton* by Kathryn Finch and Theresa Hoover

*Playing with Purpose* by Michael Matera & John Meehan

*Project-Based Learning Anywhere* by Lori Elliott

*Pure Genius* by Don Wettrick

*The Revolution* by Darren Ellwein and Derek McCoy

*The Science Box* by Kim Adsit and Adam Peterson

*Shift This!* by Joy Kirr

*Skyrocket Your Teacher Coaching* by Michael Cary Sonbert

*Spark Learning* by Ramsey Musallam

*Sparks in the Dark* by Travis Crowder and Todd Nesloney

*Table Talk Math* by John Stevens

*Teachables* by Cheryl Abla and Lisa Maxfield

*Unpack Your Impact* by Naomi O'Brien and LaNesha Tabb

*The Wild Card* by Hope and Wade King

*Writefully Empowered* by Jacob Chastain

*The Writing on the Classroom Wall* by Steve Wyborney

*You Are Poetry* by Mike Johnston

*You'll Never Guess What I'm Saying* by Naomi O'Brien

*You'll Never Guess What I'm Thinking About* by Naomi O'Brien

## Inspiration, Professional Growth & Personal Development

*Be REAL* by Tara Martin
*Be the One for Kids* by Ryan Sheehy
*The Coach ADVenture* by Amy Illingworth
*Creatively Productive* by Lisa Johnson
*The Ed Branding Book* by Dr. Renae Bryant and Lynette White
*Educational Eye Exam* by Alicia Ray
*The EduNinja Mindset* by Jennifer Burdis
*Empower Our Girls* by Lynmara Colón and Adam Welcome
*Finding Lifelines* by Andrew Grieve and Andrew Sharos
*The Four O'Clock Faculty* by Rich Czyz
*How Much Water Do We Have?* by Pete and Kris Nunweiler
*P Is for Pirate* by Dave and Shelley Burgess
*A Passion for Kindness* by Tamara Letter
*The Path to Serendipity* by Allyson Apsey
*PheMOMenal Teacher* by Annick Rauch
*Recipes for Resilience* by Robert A. Martinez
*Rogue Leader* by Rich Czyz
*Sanctuaries* by Dan Tricarico
*Saving Sycamore* by Molly B. Hudgens
*The Secret Sauce* by Rich Czyz
*Shattering the Perfect Teacher Myth* by Aaron Hogan
*Stories from Webb* by Todd Nesloney
*Talk to Me* by Kim Bearden
*Teach Better* by Chad Ostrowski, Tiffany Ott, Rae Hughart, and Jeff Gargas
*Teach Me, Teacher* by Jacob Chastain
*Teach, Play, Learn!* by Adam Peterson
*The Teachers of Oz* by Herbie Raad and Nathan Lang-Raad
*Teaching Is a Tattoo* by Mike Johnston
*Teaching the Ms. Abbott Way* by Joyce Stephens Abbott
*TeamMakers* by Laura Robb and Evan Robb
*Through the Lens of Serendipity* by Allyson Apsey
*Write Here and Now* by Dan Tricarico
*The Zen Teacher* by Dan Tricarico

## Children's Books

*The Adventures of Little Mickey* by Mickey Smith Jr.

*Alpert* by LaNesha Tabb

*Alpert & Friends* by LaNesha Tabb

*Beyond Us* by Aaron Polansky

*Cannonball In* by Tara Martin

*Dolphins in Trees* by Aaron Polansky

*Dragon Smart* by Tisha and Tommy Richmond

*I Can Achieve Anything* by MoNique Waters

*I Want to Be a Lot* by Ashley Savage

*The Magic of Wonder* by Jenna Copper, Ashley Bible, Abby Gross, and Staci Lamb

*Micah's Big Question* by Naomi O'Brien

*The Princes of Serendip* by Allyson Apsey

*Ride with Emilio* by Richard Nares

*A Teacher's Top Secret Confidential* by LaNesha Tabb

*A Teacher's Top Secret: Mission Accomplished* by LaNesha Tabb

*The Wild Card Kids* by Hope and Wade King

*Zom-Be a Design Thinker* by Amanda Fox

www.ingramcontent.com/pod-product-compliance
Lightning Source LLC
Chambersburg PA
CBHW081200230426
43666CB00016B/2874